STUFF YOU

DON'T

HAVE TO

PRAY ABOUT

SUSIE SHELLENBERGER

BROADMAN
&HOLMAN
PUBLISHERS

Nashville, Tennessee

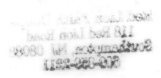

Printed in the United States of America

4250-89
0-8054-5089-0

Published by
Broadman & Holman Publishers
Nashville, Tennessee

Scripture quotations are from the Holy Bible, New International Version, © 1973, 1978, 1984 by International Bible Society; TLB, The Living Bible, © Tyndale House Publishers, Wheaton, Ill., 1971, used by permission; TEV, the Bible in Today's English Version, Old Testament © 1976, New Testament © 1966, 1971, 1976 American Bible Society, used by permission; and The Message: The New Testament in Contemporary English, © 1993 by Eugene H. Peterson, published by NavPress, Colorado Springs, Colo.

Library of Congress Cataloging-in-Publication Data

Shellenberger, Susie.
    Stuff you don't have to pray about / Susie Shellenberger.
        p. cm.
    Summary: Includes stories of contemporary teens as well as contemporary retelling of Bible stories and personal application. Each chapter lists suggestions for things for which to pray.
        ISBN 0-8054-5089-0 (pbk.)
    1. Teenagers—Religious life. 2 Prayer—Christianity—Juvenile literature. [1. Prayer. 2. Christian life.] I. Title.
BV4531.2.S48   1995
248.8'3—dc20   95-5616
                                                                            CIP
                                                                            AC

Dewey: 248.83
Subhead: YOUTH—RELIGIOUS LIFE

99 98 97 96 95 — 5 4 3 2 1

Red Lion Faith Chapel
118 Red Lion Road
Southampton, NJ 08088
609-859-2211

DEDICATED TO SUSAN WOODARD...

I was out of college and away from home for the
 first time.
 Conway, Arkansas.
 Didn't know a soul.
 Till you invited me over for dinner.

When I arrived, you led me to the table and said,
 "Susie, this will always be *your* place.
We want you to be part of our family.
This place will be set for you every single night.
If you get a better offer, or want to be alone,
 that's fine.
But your place will still be set—
 whether you come or not."

Then with growing conviction, you added,
 "Understand what I'm saying: When you come over,
 we're not going to scramble around and set your place . . .
 it will always be set.
 You're part of *us* now."

Do you have any idea how much security that gave me?
And when you hung a Christmas stocking with

my name on it above your mantle and
stuck *my* picture on your fridge with stuff
your kids made in school,
do you know how *connected* I felt?

You gave me belonging.

Though I will always smile when I think of
       Gunsmoke snacks, Crayons, and Big Chief tablets . . .
       the images I draw strength from are our prayer
       times together.
Hearts united in conversation with our Creator God.
Times we'd stay up past midnight talking
    theology
    and
    Scripture
    and
    doctrine.

Through the years and across the miles,
    I've probably told
    a million people that you're
    the most creative person I know.
But there's something that goes far beyond
your creativity.
And that's your steadfastness.
Which brings me back to our friendship.
For sixteen years you have prayed with me,
    laughed with me,
    cried with me.
Because of that steadfastness,
I know you are a friend committed to the long haul.

Thank you.

I'll meet you in Little Rock anytime.
(I have a Moped, you know.)

STUFF THAT'S IN THIS BOOK

READ THIS FIRST!

I had just moved to Colorado Springs and had barely unpacked my bags and arranged my furniture when a staff member from one of the local churches I had visited gave me a call. "Look, Susie," he said. "I'm coming straight to the point. We're glad you're here, but I hope you're not wanting to wait until you get settled before getting involved at church. We desperately need to start a new Sunday School class for young adults. Will you teach it?"

I told him I'd love to; I didn't even need to pray about it.

A few months later when the youth minister approached me about some teens in the youth group, he said, "I have five high schoolers who really need to be grounded in the Bible. Could you have them over to your place once a week and disciple them?"

"Sure," I said. "I don't even need to pray about it."

How could I say I knew what God wanted me to do without having to ask Him? Because God's Word makes it clear that He has given us spiritual gifts that we are to use for Him (see Romans 12:6–8). I know God has given me the spiritual gift of teaching. So, when asked if I would teach a class of adults and disciple a small group of teens, I already knew what God wanted me to do. I didn't need to ask Him about the decision. He had already made His will clear by revealing to me the specific areas in which He had gifted me.

You see, there are some things we just don't need to bathe in prayer. Why? Because God has already settled several issues in His Word. To continue going over the same old ground only prevents spiritual growth.

I believe you are reading this book because you want to deepen your relationship with the Lord. In other words, instead of praying about the same ol' things, you want to move on to other exciting areas of spiritual growth. Often, though, it's hard to realize what areas we *don't* need to spend time praying about. Use this book as a guide to move you away from redundant chitchat conversations with your Father and into an ever-deepening, powerful prayer life with the Creator of the universe!

God dreams B-I-G dreams for you! (Check out Ephesians 3:20 for proof.) So spend your time and energy growing into all He wants you to become!

Susie

1

Taking a Stand

Instead of calling him Mr. President, they called him King. His real name was King Nebuchadnezzar, but most people called him "King Nebbie Babie." KNB was stuck on himself. He had such a huge ego that he contracted the Sizzling Sculpture Guys to create a solid gold, ninety-foot statue of himself.

On the day of its completion, KNB decided to mark the unveiling with a great celebration. He announced the world's first, largest, and loudest rock concert.

Then, he passed a law that forced every citizen to attend his bash. It was massive! They had amps lined up the distance of a football field. And anyone who was anywhere on the music charts was there.

KNB grabbed the mike and announced the party rules. "When the jam starts to flow, I want everyone to do the new national dance I've created. I'm calling it 'The Bow.' As we unveil my ninety-foot golden replica, the music will crank and you'll bow. Got it?"

Thousands nodded their empty heads in agreement. The jam flowed. The golden giant glistened in the sun as it was carefully unveiled. KNB eyed his citizens swaying and bowing to the new national dance. They all bowed—literally thousands. All of them.

OK. Some of you have heard the story before (it's found in Daniel 3). You know that three didn't bow. Young men. Teenagers, actually. You know their names . . . Shad, Mad, and Bad. There they stood, refusing to bow.

KNB was furious! He grabbed the mic again and spit out the rules. "We're cranking up the tunes. When you hear the music, bend those knees. If you don't do 'The Bow,' you'll be tossed into this fiery furnace."

They cranked. You know how it sounds when you can *feel* the music? (This usually happens when your parents have left the house. It's so loud you can actually feel the ground beneath you vibrate.) This music was sooooo loud, it was way past that. It was electric. (It's important you understand just how LOUD this music was.) It was SO LOUD, it personified itself. (That means it took on human characteristics. We'll cover metaphors and similes later.)

Not only could you *hear* it. You could *taste* it as the notes slid down your throat. You could *smell* the rhythm as it throbbed against your body. You could *see* the beat wrapping itself around your life. And you could *feel* the chords as they danced through your soul. Ooooh. It was w-i-l-d—like you became ONE with the music.

Thousands bowed. But Shad, Mad, and Bad continued to stand. Tall. Head and shoulders above the rest. (That's what happens when you take a stand for God . . . you stand head and shoulders above EVERYONE. But if you don't stand for God, you'll fall for everything the world tosses your way.)

KNB was livid! He brought them right down front where everyone could see. And then he . . . well, tell you what. Let me communicate this story in a more modern way. Let's listen in on the conversation between KNB and Shad. I'll narrate. Somebody get a beat going for me. I bet it would've sounded something like this:

"Yo, Guards! A way back there
I see three young men givin' *me* the stare!

"Whassa prob? Don't they know what to do?
Sway their bodies to the music, do a little soft shoe?
Lissen up, boys, standin' in the back,
You makin' King Nebbie Babie, really really hacked!
Standin' back there with your heads held high
As if you don't believe me when I say YOU GONNA DIE!

"So come on now, join in the fun,
Music's playin' loud, we be dancin' in the sun.
What? You worried that it's not too clean?
Chill out dudes! It's the party machine!
Jam's pumpin' fast and it's happin' now
This is *my* fling, and *I* say DO THE BOW!"

Well, Shad spoke up, that brave young man
Looked around, said, **"Whoa! I'm takin' a stand.
Yo, King! Mister, Mister
I tune in to God. Not *you*, Twisted Sister!
I serve a God who is mighty and holy,
His angels sing better than *even* Bon Jovi.
His Word is true, all those Bible stories
Not like the lies handed down from Beastie Boys.
King Nebbie, you actin' like a fool
Got 'em tryin' to dance like Paula Abdul.
You know—Jesus *is* the Solid Rock
So we kicked those New Kids off the block!
Your lack of faith is such a loss
You jammin' to dweebs like Kris Kross.
They can't even put their clothes on straight
You think they're gonna lead you to the Holy Gate?
You're goin' to Heaven; your ticket's been bought**

3

You're a good guy; God just forgot.
NOT!

"You livin' in sin, and it's makin' you dead
While you do the mosh pit with the Lemmonheads!
Your mouth's hangin' open, you gawkin' at Madonna
You dressin' in grunge and swingin' with Nirvana.

"I'm here to tell, and I'm in your face
My cues come from God, not Ace of Base.
KNB, you ain't gonna win
Till you learn to disciple your Boys II Men.

"See anger + hate = one big riot
But that's whatcha get with the Stone Temple Pilots!
Jesus Christ is true—He will never fail
Now you can't say THAT about Nine Inch Nails.

"You think you're cool cuz you got Green Day
Didja know their opening act is a band that's gay?
Pansy Division—that's their name
If ya ask me, I think they're *all* pretty lame!
Someday I'll meet the saints, I'll even talk to Moses
I'll eat the bread of life—but not with Guns 'N' Roses."

King said, "Repeat! In case you didn't hear
Lissen to the rules. Am I makin' myself clear?
We crankin' up the heat. In the fire you gonna boil."

Shad says, **"That's OK. I got my Coppertone Oil!"**
"Shut your face smart boy. Don't gimme no lip."

"Hey, I know God. Therefore I am hip!
He's even King over you, His power much higher
He's seen me through the storm, and
He'll take me through the fire."

Well, Shad, Mad, and Bad were thrown into the furnace.
And the King heard 'em scream **"Your fire won't burn us!"**

Those words made the King *extremely* sore
But as he leaned a little closer, you know he saw the Lord?

"Let this be a lesson, King Nebbie," said He.
"You come out a winner when you take a stand for Me!"

* * *

You know what happened, don't you? KNB leaned over the edge of that big fiery furnace and screamed, "Hey!" (Man of great vocabulary.) "I threw *three* men into that pit. Who's the fourth guy?"

"He is our GOD," Bad said. "And He will NEVER leave us!" shouted Mad.

Those three young men, Shadrach, Meshach, and Abednego, were thrown into the fire, but God didn't forsake them. And He won't forsake you, either. He promised.

FEELIN' THE HEAT?

You might feel like you're in a fiery furnace right now. Maybe some students at school are making fun of you because of your faith. Perhaps you're being pressured to drink, cheat, or become sexually involved. It's comforting to know that God is already committed to be with you. You don't have to ask Him to show up. He's already there. And He doesn't expect you to stand by yourself. Christ promised to be your strength and to hold you up while you stand.

Repeat after me: *If I don't take a stand for Christ, I'll fall for everything. But when I stand for HIM, I stand head and shoulders above everyone else.*

Funny. At the beginning of the story, three young men stood at the back of the crowd. But because they continued to stand in the midst of pressure, God moved them right down front. The statue? No one seemed to notice anymore. Even ninety feet of solid gold pales when three godly teens stand in front of it.

STUFF YOU DON'T HAVE TO PRAY ABOUT

Taking a stand isn't always easy, is it? Sometimes it hurts to go against the crowd. Yet, when we're confronted with something we know is morally wrong, unethical, or something that will interfere in our walk with Christ, we know He wants us to stand tall. We don't need to ask.

We don't serve a God who says, "Stand up! I'll check on you next week to see how you're doing." No way. The same God who calls you to stand, *holds you up*. He's not bailing out on you. He's in the furnace with you. And yes, He feels the heat too!

"Happy are all who search for God, and always do his will, REJECTING COMPROMISE with evil, and walking only in his paths" (Psalm 119:2–3, TLB, caps mine).

STUFF YOU SHOULD PRAY ABOUT

No need to waste time praying about whether to take a stand. Instead, spend some time praying for:

1. Courage. When you're the only one in health class who disagrees with the "safe sex" lie, seek His boldness to speak out.

Ammunition: Joshua 1:5–9. What is God commanding of you? What does He promise you in return?

When we lack confidence, we struggle with new challenges God wants to bring our way. That's how Jeremiah felt. He was about your age, and God wanted him to stand tall and speak out. Listen to their conversation:

"'O Lord God,' I said, 'I can't do that! I'm far too young! I'm only a youth!'

'Don't say that,' he replied, 'for you will go wherever I send you and speak whatever I tell you to. And don't

6

be afraid of the people, for I, the Lord, will be with you and see you through' "(Jeremiah 1:6–8, TLB).

2. Strength. When you take a stand and feel attacked, seek His power to continue standing—even on shaky legs.

Ammunition: Hebrews 12:12–13, TLB. What does God say about being shaky? Absorb 1 Peter 5:10–11. Catch the promise? It's for you!

> **Father,** I know You understand what I go through at school, because You know everything. I guess sometimes I just need to be reminded that You feel the heat with me.
>
> To be honest, sometimes I just get really scared. I don't wanna be labeled as a dweeb. I get too caught up in wanting to be cool and worrying about what others will think.
>
> Lord, help me to focus more on being Your voice in my world. Thanks for promising to never leave me. Help me to trust You more. Show me specific ways that I can take a stand tomorrow. Amen.

2

THE VICTORY RACE

I played four years of varsity tennis in college. I had a lazy habit of standing flat-footed on the court while waiting for the serve to sail over the net. I can remember hearing my coach's instructions through the fence and across the line-up of courts. "On your toes, Shellenberger!" she'd yell. "Get on your toes!"

She knew that to win I had to have a specific plan. And part of that plan had to be reflected in the way I played. Standing flat-footed kept me from being as ready as I needed to be to receive the serve.

If you watch professional tennis on TV, you'll notice that the athlete who's preparing to receive the serve is *always* on his toes. In fact, he usually jumps slightly, right before the ball sails over the net. That's part of his plan. He's ready! Successful tennis requires good strategy . . . as does anything in life that's worth attempting.

SPIRITUAL SUCCESS

Many of us don't realize that to some degree, this principle also holds true in our spiritual lives. If we want to be spiritually successful (live victoriously), we need to set certain truths in motion. In other words, we need to *plan* for spiritual consistency. We won't just evolve into mature godly giants.

The Apostle Paul asks a penetrating question in Galatians 5:7: "You were getting along so well. Who has interfered with you to hold you back from following the truth. It certainly isn't God who has done it, for he is the one who has called you to freedom in Christ. But it takes only one wrong person among you to infect all the others" (TLB).

Where are you right now, spiritually? Doing well? Or did you *used to be* doing well?

What's your strategy? How do you plan to do well spiritually? How do you plan to keep up your spiritual victory? How can you live *consistently* with victory in your life?

Again, you need a strategy. A GOOD strategy. You need a strategy to win. A solid game plan.

COACH PETER SAYS...

The Apostle Peter presents a winning combination. If we follow this specific strategy, we're making plans to live victoriously on a daily basis. Let's take a peek at what he says.

> Do you want more and more of God's kindness and peace? Then learn to know him better and better. For as you know him better, he will give you, through his great power, everything you need for living a truly good life: he even shares his own glory and his own goodness with us! And by that same mighty power he has given us all the other rich and wonderful blessings he promised; for instance, the promise to save us from the lust and rottenness all around us, and to give us his own character.

> But to obtain these gifts, you need more than faith; you must also work hard to be good, and even that is not enough. For then you must learn to know God better and discover what he wants you to do. Next, learn to

put aside your own desires so that you will become patient and godly, gladly letting God have his way with you. This will make possible the next step, which is for you to enjoy other people and to like them, and finally you will grow to love them deeply. The more you go on in this way, the more you will grow strong spiritually and become fruitful and useful to our Lord Jesus Christ (2 Peter 1:2–8, TLB).

The Christian life has been compared to a race (see 1 Corinthians 9:24–27), so let's just pretend that the Apostle Peter is our coach. We're headed out for a track meet, and he's in the locker room with us going over the three points in our strategy.

#1: LEARN TO KNOW GOD BETTER AND BETTER

In order to run quickly and consistently on the track, you have to know your event. If you're a sprinter, you'll run differently than a long-distance runner will. You learn to pace yourself, and you'll find out all you can about your area of competition.

In order to run the race of Christianity with victory, you find out all you can about your Creator. He, in turn, will guide and mold you to be the best "runner" or disciple you can be.

I used to be a public high school teacher. I taught speech, drama, and English. Each year my students would go through the process of getting to know me. They realized the better they knew me, the more they knew what to expect on tests, homework assignments, and class environment. They knew their success in class, to a degree, depended on how well they learned what the teacher expected.

The same principle applies to our spiritual lives. That's why Peter tells us to get to know the Lord better and better. It's not just a once-in-a-while get-together. It's a continual getting to know Him. And as we know Him better, we begin to understand Him more. THAT'S when we reap the benefits (power, joy, security) of His friendship.

Getting to know someone takes active effort on your part, doesn't it? When you establish a friendship with someone, you're anxious to talk with them, and you look forward to spending time with him or her. It works the same way in your relationship with Christ. To know the Lord intimately requires some action and work on your part. You must develop a relationship with Him—just as you would with a human friend.

The book *Twelve and One-Half Keys* by Edward Hays tells the story of an innocent man who was unjustly sentenced to prison. He was a poor, yet honest, jeweler and a devout, godly man. After he had been imprisoned for several months, his wife visited with the guards and showed them a rug. "It's his prayer rug," she explained. "He's lost without it. Could he just have this one possession?"

The guards agreed that a small rug would not do anyone any harm and consented to allowing him to have it. Several weeks passed, and the jeweler presented an interesting proposition to the guards. "I'm bored sitting here all day long with nothing to do," he said. "If you'll grant me a few scraps of metal and a couple of simple tools, I'll make jewelry for you. I just want to be able to keep up my trade. You can sell what I make for your own profit."

The overworked and underpaid guards quickly agreed to the arrangement, and each day brought him a few scraps of metal and some tools. Then, each night, they would take the tools away from him and sell what he had made for their own profit.

Months later, when the guards approached his cell one morning, they saw he was gone. The door was locked; there was no sign of forced entry; and there were absolutely no clues. It seemed as if he just disappeared!

Later, the man who had actually committed the crime was found and sent to prison. Long afterward one of the guards saw the innocent man's wife at the city market. He quickly explained that the criminal was behind bars, but wanted to know what had happened to her husband.

She told the guard that she had gone to the main architect—the one who had actually designed the prison. She obtained from him the blueprints of the cell doors and locks. Then she wove the design into a prayer rug. Each day as her husband knelt and bowed to pray, his head touched the rug. Gradually, he began to see that there was a design inside a design inside another design inside yet another design, and he finally figured out that it was the design to the lock of his cell.

From small bits of leftover metal, he created a key and simply unlocked his own door, walked out of the cell, then shut the door again!

The first part of your strategy for a victorious Christian life is to know your Creator as well as you can. Like interpreting the design on a rug, it takes study, discipline, and consistency. But it's a plan that will move you toward a joyous relationship with Him.

#2: Follow His Strategy, Not Your Own

Again, if you're competing in a track meet, one of your top priorities is to carry out the instructions your coach has given you. One runner told me her coach had suggested that she hold her fingers a certain way when she ran. When I asked her what she was talking about, she explained, "He told me to run as if I'm holding a dime between my thumb and first finger. I hold each hand this way the entire time I am running."

"Why?" I said. "What's that accomplish?"

"If I don't hold my fingers this way, my hands just sort of flop around when I run. This gives me a specific thing to do with them and helps me focus more intently on what I'm doing."

Hmmm. Makes sense. It also made sense that she didn't argue with her coach or try to talk him into a plan *she* had created.

We must have a strategy in order to live a victorious Christian life. It's important that we adopt HIS strategy for winning, and not our own. After all, our Creator knows far better than we do what we're up against, what our future holds, and how we can be victorious.

The more time you spend with your Heavenly Father, the clearer His strategy for your life will become. The key is (like the key in getting to know Him better) spending time in prayer and reading His personal letter to you (the Bible). As you get to know Him better and better, His Holy Spirit will reveal His truth to you on a daily basis.

#3: BE AN ENCOURAGER

When you're competing in a track meet, it always helps to see and hear people on the sidelines (and in the stands) cheering you on. That little extra encouragement many times can affect the outcome of a race.

In our walk with God, we too, need to be cheered on by our Christian friends. It makes a difference to know someone is praying for you, doesn't it? And when you receive a card or note in the mail from a church member explaining that you were missed last Sunday, it feels good.

Likewise, to be consistently victorious in your relationship with God, you need to be an encourager. PLAN to cheer others on. Affirm those around you. Find the good things in others and focus your attention on those positive qualities. Build each other up. Put your arm around someone. Make a phone call. Sit with a visitor at your church. All these things add up to *making a difference* in someone's life. That, in turn, helps YOU maintain your own spiritual consistency.

Again, like (1) getting to know God and, (2) learning His strategy for your life, (3) being an encourager requires action! It's hard work . . . but it's necessary to becoming all God wants you to be.

We live in a world that encourages sarcasm. Every TV sitcom is filled with dialogue laced with fast come-backs, sarcastic one-liners, and quick put-downs. It has become not only accept-ed for us to be sarcastic and short with others, but it's also become expected. Breaking that mold will require active think-ing, doing, and being on your part. It's much easier to put people down in a joking manner than it is to build them up.

But guess who the victorious people are? You're right! They're the ones who have made a HABIT of affirming those around them. Think about it: Who do you absolutely love being around? People who make you feel good about yourself, right?

Every time you help someone else feel worthwhile, it all comes back to you. God, in turn, affirms *you* and sets you on that streak of spiritual victory.

Again, this requires conscious action. A few years ago, Christian contemporary singer Steven Curtis Chapman cut a music video called *The Great Adventure*. I was invited to join the cast and crew for the making of the video while interviewing Steven for a magazine cover story.

We shot in the Grand Teton Mountains in Jackson Hole, Wyoming. I had a bit part as an extra in the video. It was my job to sit on the side of a fence and toss a cowboy hat in the air. I'm in the video three times, but if you blink, you'll miss me.

Now, granted that was really a teeny-tiny role. Steven, of course, had the major part. After all, it was his video. He obvi-ously had a lot on his mind—cues to remember, camera angles, words to the song, etc. Yet he still took the time to stop and encourage *me*—an extra in a small, bit role.

As I watched him throughout the shoot, I saw Steven doing the same thing with other crew members: the stylist who applied his makeup, the person who cut his hair, the wardrobe personnel. For Steven, being an encourager is a way of life. He has devel-oped a healthy habit of affirming those around him; it has almost become second nature.

That's part of being "Jesus" to our world, isn't it? And as we reflect Him . . . again, we're planning for spiritual victory.

STUFF YOU DON'T HAVE TO PRAY ABOUT

Do you need to spend time praying about how you can attain spiritual victory? Nope. God has already outlined His plan. He's already given you a specific strategy to follow.

God wants you to be spiritually successful *even more than you do*. He died for your spiritual victory. But it won't happen by running the Christian race carelessly without aim or purpose. We have to *plan* to be successful.

STUFF YOU SHOULD PRAY ABOUT

Instead of praying about how to live victoriously, focus your prayers on:

1. Being an infector. Remember that verse in Galatians we started out with? "You were getting along so well. Who has interfered with you to hold you back from following the truth? It certainly isn't God who has done it, for he is the one who has called you to freedom in Christ. But it takes only one wrong person among you to infect all the others" (5:7).

You're either infected (you used to do well spiritually, but have fallen back), or you're an infector. If you're infected, seek God's forgiveness and move forward.

If you're an infector, you're either infecting others in a POSITIVE way or a NEGATIVE way. If you're the one who's always complaining, bringing disharmony to your youth group, being negative, exhibiting pride or selfishness, then it doesn't take a genius to figure out that you're infecting those around you in a harmful way. (It only takes one, remember?)

If you're infecting in a positive manner, then you're spreading love and affirmation to those around you. Determine to be a positive infector. (It only takes one, remember?) What a huge difference you can make in your school and youth group!

Ammunition: 1 Timothy 4:7–10 says some strong things about infectors. And check out 1 Timothy 4:12. In fact, let this become your motto. What does this say about the influence you can have on others?

2. Being an imitator. "Your attitude should be the kind that was shown us by Jesus Christ, who, though he was God, did not demand and cling to his rights as God, but laid aside his mighty power and glory, taking the disguise of a slave and becoming like men" (Philippians 2:5–7, TLB).

When striving for spiritual victory, who's your perfect example? Spend time imitating Him.

Ammunition: Ephesians 5:1–2. What happens when you imitate your heavenly Father?

3. Living out the strategy. If you're not spiritually victorious, it's probably because you're not actively following God's plan for spiritual victory. So let's review the strategy:

#1: Learn to know Him better and better.

#2: Follow HIS strategy, not your own.

#3: Be an encourager.

Ammunition: Your strategy is specifically explained in 2 Peter 1:2–8. Follow each step for attaining and maintaining spiritual victory.

Father, I confess that many times I don't really think about HOW to live in spiritual victory . . . I either just expect it to happen, or I wonder why I'm not spiritually successful.

Thanks for helping me realize that I need a plan. And thanks for not making me create my own plan, but for giving me YOUR plan—all lined out in steps I can understand.

Give me the desire and the discipline I need to follow
YOUR strategy. In faith, I thank You ahead of time
for the spiritual victory that's mine. Amen.

STUFF TO GROW ON #1

Having trouble understanding God's Word? Then get a Bible you can understand. There are several choices for teens. Check out the following options at a local Christian bookstore:

• *Life Application Bible* (Tyndale). This one's packed with everything you need to zap your spiritual life in a mega way. Every page has some "handle" to pull you into the Word. It's like a magnet and feels like something you *want* to read.

Highlights: reading plans for daily devotions, biblical answers to hot-button questions about God, straightforward insights on moral dilemmas, advice from teens, and lots of cool charts, maps, and graphics.

• *Serendipity Bible for Students* (Zondervan). If you belong to a Bible study or want to *start* a Bible study, this is the Bible you need. It's absolutely stashed with creative questions in the margins, designed to challenge your thinking and deepen your walk with God. The serendipity questions also move you to look more intimately within *yourself*.

Highlights: ideas for creative group activities listed at the beginning of each chapter (to get everyone excited about the particular study), historical background profiles, options for Bible-reading plans (example: 7-week plan, 13-week plan, preliminary reading, etc.), and three different levels of spiritual challenge: open, dig, and reflect.

• *YouthWalk Devotional Bible* (Zondervan). Lots of "Hot Topics" jammed into this one. You'll get hooked reading those, and before you know it, you're into the Scripture. This one doesn't have as many notes as some of the others, but it's definitely worth checking out.

Highlights: The "Hot Topics" sections in this Bible are the pull. A few of the "Hot Topics" you'll focus on are: "What Is Hell Like?" "Why the Bible Is Reliable," "What About Suffering?"

• *The New Student Bible* (Zondervan). There's no way you can read THIS and not understand what God is saying. It's full of helpful explanations and "Insights" to get you into the Word. For instance, at the beginning of the book of Job, you'll find "What Not to Say to a Hurting Person" with an imaginary situation that places you in a hospital room with a close friend.

Highlights: subject guide, introduction to each book, insight section, list of highlights that explain confusing verses and point out interesting facts that could easily be overlooked.

The three-track reading plan helps students who want to get into the habit of daily devotion but struggle with discipline. Readers are started out on an easy track of five minutes per day.

• *The One Minute Bible 4 Students* (Garborgs). This isn't a complete Bible. It's a *devotional* Bible . . . meaning it's stocked with 365 daily readings with a lot of splashy notes. It's hard to put this one down simply because of the cool graphics inside. It's as fun to look at as it is to read.

Highlights: the notes and the graphics.

Is that all? Nope. There are several youth Bibles on the market today. Skim through the following list for a few more, but be sure to check with your local Christian bookstore for the full scoop!

• *InStep Student Bible* (Nelson). Available in Contemporary English Version.

• *Recovery Devotional Bible* (Zondervan). Great for those who are "overcoming." Includes 365 daily readings.

• *The Message* (NavPress). It's not a translation—it's a paraphrase. More modern than *The Living Bible*.

• *The Teen Study Bible* (Zondervan). This one's specifically geared to ages 12-16.

• *The Youth Bible* (Word/Group). Available in the New Century Version.

• *Time with God* (Word). This is a one-year devotional Bible in the New Testament only.

But there's *still* more! If you're into computers, you may be interested in studying the Bible with some exciting software that's now available. Here's a short list, but again, check with your local Christian bookstore for more information.

Bible Master 3.0	PC Study Bible 3.0
BibleSource 2.0	Quick Verse 2.0
Logos 1.6	WORDsearch
macBible 3.0	

3

COOL, COOLER, COOLEST

For good or bad, families have a deep impact on their children. Whether you realize it or not, you're being influenced *right now* by your family. And someday, you'll have an impact on your own family. Specific qualities and characteristics are often passed down from generation to generation. Your priorities will determine whether or not you pass along traits that enhance or destroy others.

I don't think King Herod ever got that message. Throughout his family history, his kids, his grandkids, his great-grandkids, and even his nephews were all concerned about one major thing—looking cool—and it all began with Grandpa Herod himself (Herod the Great).

Each generation was consumed with wanting more power, looking good in front of the crowds, and making their mark in history. Each followed the other in weaknesses, mistakes, and missed opportunities to do the right thing. Check out the havoc they created:

23

- Herod the Great murdered Bethlehem's children.
- Herod Antipas was slightly involved in the trial of Jesus and had John the Baptist executed.
- Herod Agrippa I murdered the Apostle James.
- Herod Agrippa II was a sarcastic judge involved in the Apostle Paul's trial.

AIRING DIRTY LAUNDRY

Let's focus our attention on Herod Antipas. He had an opportunity that most of us would love to have. He got to meet Jesus face to face . . . but he failed to recognize who Jesus was. Let's back up a bit and soak in the details that led to that encounter.

It doesn't feel good to have someone notice your faults, does it? We all have them, but most of us either try to keep them hidden or strive to change our weaknesses into strengths. Herod wanted to hide his sins, but he couldn't. Everyone knew what was going on. You see, he divorced his wife so he could marry his brother's wife, Herodias. Not a smart move, but he had power so he thought he could get away with it.

John the Baptist had been holding some desert revivals and thousands had come to hear him. Good preaching is always filled with stories and examples, right? And guess what story John used to illustrate sin? Herod and Herodias.

You can imagine how ticked off Herodias was! Herod wasn't too happy about it either, but he liked John. Apparently this desert preacher was the only one who really told it like it was to Herod. Though he never liked what he heard, Herod liked that he heard the truth.

But Herod couldn't have John keep telling the people what a sinful leader they had. And Herodias was REALLY pressuring him to silence the guy. Yet Herod was afraid to have John killed, so Herod put him in prison.

Seemed like an easy solution, and remember, Herod didn't want conflict. This was the guy who wanted everyone to like him. He had to look cool in front of the crowds.

THE BIRTHDAY BASH

That took care of things for a while, but Herodias was still steamed. She finally got her chance to do something about it, though, at Herod's birthday party.

This was a major event. Herod actually gave the party for himself. It was a stag party for his palace aides, army officers, and the leading citizens of Galilee. (Big crowd!) The wine flowed freely, lots of snacks. (You know, those little, bitty weinies stuffed in tiny biscuits served with mustard—stuff like that.)

He had hired Herodias' daughter to dance for all his male friends. (I guess if you're going to pay someone, you might as well keep the money in the family, right?) And this was no country line dance she was doing. Neither was it anything someone could do aerobically. This dance was sin in action. Rhythmic wickedness. Vile filth in slow motion.

You can imagine how the drunken men reacted. They screamed for more. Herod was so proud of himself for looking cool in front of all his male friends, he arrogantly boasted, "That was . . . wow. I mean, that was really . . . hey . . . you're hot! As an extra bonus, I'll give you anything you ask for."

He assumed she'd ask for a small piece of the kingdom or a few material possessions. Instead, though, she left the stage and found mom. "What should I ask for?" she said. "They're all drunk. Help me think of something really big!"

Herodias had already been thinking. "Tell Herod you want him to kill John the Baptist."

"Kill him?"

"Yeah. But let's make it interesting. Tell him you want John's head delivered to you on a platter!"

25

Yeah, that was big all right. Herodias' daughter climbed back on stage and grabbed the mic. A hush fell over the crowd, and the room was silenced. She announced in full detail what her mom had planted in her mind. Herod's face fell. *Kill John? Serve his head on a platter?* Not only was that an atrocity—it was depraved!

He quickly scanned the room. Drunken men began to cheer and howl. How could he disappoint his guests? He had to keep their approval. He had to look cool. He would have been embarrassed to back down now.

So, though he hated doing it, Herod demanded John's head on a platter. He had caved in . . . but he still looked cool in the eyes of his friends. Still, I imagine Herod didn't sleep much that night.

STILL MAKING BAD DECISIONS

A few months later, he met Jesus. Herod immediately associated Jesus with John because they were cousins. Again, Herod found himself in an awkward position. He didn't know what to do with Jesus. He didn't want to make the same mistakes he had made with John, yet he didn't want to take the action necessary to turn from his sins. That wouldn't look cool. His friends might not accept him any more.

Not knowing what else to do, he tried to threaten Jesus just before His last journey to Jerusalem. When he met with Jesus during one of His final trials, Jesus wouldn't even speak to him. Herod hadn't listened to John, and Christ didn't have anything else to add to His cousin's words. Herod's heart had been hardened. Because he had rejected God's message, he found it easy to reject God Himself in the form of Jesus Christ. His response to Jesus' silence? Herod mocked Him.

Herod met Jesus! If only he would have recognized Him for who He really was. But for years Herod had made choices to look cool in front of the crowd, and his heart had hardened so that he couldn't recognize Jesus.

Herod could have turned his dysfunctional family history right side up. He *could* have influenced all of Galilee to follow God and spread the Gospel. But being cool was more important.

STUFF YOU DON'T HAVE TO PRAY ABOUT

Everyone loves to be loved. It's normal. In fact, God placed this desire within you. And guess what? You've had it since birth.

If you're not receiving enough love, attention, and positive affirmation from your family, chances are you'll try to find it in other ways such as standing on the cafeteria table and sticking French fries up an underclassman's nose, being the class clown, putting someone down before they get a chance to get to you, or hiding your fetal pig from biology class in Clyde Throemore's locker.

Truth is, *things and actions* don't make you cool. *Lifestyle and relationships* do. A growing relationship with Christ results in a magnetic-hard-to-resist lifestyle. And THAT'S cool!

So do you really need to spend time praying about how to become more accepted? Or cool? Or more popular? Nah. Only one kind of cool counts. Only one kind of hip has eternal value—and that's becoming all God wants you to be.

STUFF YOU DON'T HAVE TO PRAY ABOUT

Settled. No need to waste time praying about becoming cool. Instead, spend some time praying about:

1. Becoming a SHINING STAR. Don't be obsessed with being popular because God has a much higher calling on your life. Herod lived in a world darkened by sin. He could have shone brightly.

We, too, live in that same darkened world. Your blackboard jungle is filled with teens who don't need one more cool friend. They NEED someone (like John the Baptist) who will shine brightly with God's truth.

How can you do that? By refusing to go along with the crowd just to look cool. Ask God to keep your heart tender, so you won't become hardened to His voice like Herod did.

Ammunition: Philippians 2:14–16. What does God challenge you to do? When you accept His challenge, how are your friends affected?

2. Living in love. Rather than having you settle for fleeting popularity and acceptance from the crowd, God wants you to be saturated with something long-lasting and genuine: love.

Ammunition: 1 Corinthians 13:1–5. What is God's major call on your life? What are some of the things that pale in the light of love?

3. Transforming your image. When you determine to set a higher goal than popularity for yourself, you won't be able to look to your friends for the example on how to live your life. Look instead at God's Word. It's jammed-packed with powerful examples of people who answered God's higher calling on their lives.

Ammunition: Romans 12:2–3. According to these verses, what are you challenged *not* to do? How does this relate with trying to be cool? Based on this Scripture, how can you know and understand what God wants for you?

> Lord, I really DO want to be all You call me to be. Sometimes, though, I get paranoid about what others think. And instead of focusing on my relationship with You, I become obsessed with gaining their approval. Then I do things I shouldn't just to get attention.
>
> Transform me, Lord, in YOUR image. I want to shine like a star to those around me. Help my world to see *You* in my life. Amen.

4

NOW HIRING: ACME CONSTRUCTION COMPANY

Nehemiah was an outstanding basketball player. In fact, he was on a full athletic scholarship at Galilean Community College. He was also a strong leader on campus and was enjoying his junior year as student body president.

One of his friends, a high school senior from his hometown of Jerusalem, came to visit him and look over the campus during spring break. Nehemiah was ecstatic to see his old pal, and over a coke and large order of fries at the Golden Galilean Arches, he casually asked how things were "back home."

Putting down the coke and straightening in his chair, the friend replied, "Well, things are not good; the wall of Jerusalem is still torn down, and the gates are burned" (Nehemiah 1:3, TLB).

KNOW WHAT IT FEELS LIKE?

The Bible tells us that Nehemiah was so disturbed by the shocking news that he cried. During the next several days, he refused to eat. Instead, he poured out his heart in prayer to God.

Maybe *you've* been in a crisis situation similar to Nehemiah's. You know what it feels like to be so bothered about something that to even consider eating seems like an absurdity because food is the last thing on your mind.

Nehemiah was worried about his hometown. I can imagine what that feels like. I live in Colorado Springs, but my hometown is Oklahoma City. When my mom called in tears just moments after the bombing of the Oklahoma City Federal Building on April 19, 1995, I wanted to fly home and make sure my friends and loved ones were okay.

That's what Nehemiah wanted to do. His high school buddy informed him that the walls surrounding the city were down. The city wall was important. As long as a strong, sturdy wall was intact, the people inside were safe from enemy attacks. When the wall stood high, it also meant that the spiritual condition of the people was sturdy as well. *The wall* symbolized not only a *physical* wall of strength and protection, but also a wall of *righteousness*. That wall was important!

THE WORK BEGINS

Nehemiah had a great off-campus job. He worked part-time for the king. Most kings would kill for a worker like him. He always punched in on time, never took more than fifteen minutes for a coffee break, and gave terrific visitor tours around the palace.

No wonder his employer took a special liking to him.

Noticing that the boy was a little down, the king asked if anything was wrong. Nehemiah replied, "My hometown is a wreck! The gates have been burned and the wall that surrounds the city is down. Sir, that's my city—my family and my friends! Could I have an indefinite leave of absence to go home and help restore the city wall?"

The king must have had a bowl of Cheerios that morning because he responded cheerfully and quickly granted Nehemiah's request. Nehemiah packed his bags, walking away from his basketball scholarship, his great paying job, and his student council position to return home and rebuild the wall. The rebuilding of the wall became the most important thing in his life.

Nehemiah immediately went on a Jerusalem television network and announced that he was forming a volunteer construction company to rebuild the wall of righteousness. He hit the radio stations and even put flyers underneath windshield wipers of cars in shopping mall parking lots. Nehemiah finally recruited a good group of volunteer workers and set them to task.

Meanwhile, the neighboring governors, Sanballat and Tobiah, heard about what was going on and began making plans to thwart the construction work. With the wall down, Sanballat and Tobiah had free reign to walk in and out of the city, flaunting their wickedness and working to sway the citizens to their own twisted political views. They knew if the wall was rebuilt, their influence over the people within the city would end. So they tried to distract and discourage the workers by hurling verbal insults at them.

"Hey, Nehemiah! Where'd you get your construction license—out of a Cracker Jacks box?"

"You call *that* thing a wall? I've seen stronger stuff built out of Legos!"

"Nehemiah, my *grandmother* could build stronger walls than *that!*"

Nehemiah warned his men not to stop. "Don't pay any attention to Sanballat and Tobiah. We are doing the most important thing in the world—rebuilding the wall of righteousness. We will *not* stop!"

Sticks and Stones

When Sanballat and Tobiah realized the insults weren't going to distract them, they decided to use an all-out physical attack. They began firing arrows and hurling stones at the crew.

Nehemiah, calmly downing a Twinkie, instructed half of the men to deck themselves in the armor of God while standing guard against the enemy's attacks, and the other half to continue building the wall.

It didn't take Sanballat and Tobiah long to realize that God's armor couldn't be penetrated, so they put their heads together and came up with the master plans A, B, C, and D.

The next morning they implemented Plan A. As the men were arriving for work, Sanballat and Tobiah set up a lemonade stand right across the street from the construction site. Glowing with all the fake charm they could gather, they tried to entice the men with cold drinks.

"Listen guys, I know we gave you a hard time the other day, but we realize now what a super job you're doing for your city. And to show our admiration, we're offering you complimentary glasses of lemonade anytime you want it during this hot, scorching, humid day."

Nehemiah quickly instructed his men not to stop for *anything*. So they worked consistently, and the two neighboring governors got waterlogged from trying to drink twenty-five gallons of hot, pink lemonade.

Sanballat and Tobiah were forced to go to Plan B. The next morning, after Acme Brick Company delivered a fresh supply of bricks for the wall, the two governors invited Nehemiah and his men to a "special dinner."

"Look, Nehemiah . . . we admire the work you're doing; we really do. And to show our appreciation for a job well done, we want you and your entire crew to be our guests of honor at a barbecued rib party tonight right after you punch out for the day."

Well, that sounded good! The construction crew was always tired and hungry at the end of the day, and barbecued ribs tickled their taste buds. Nehemiah's instructions to his men, however, were firm. "Men, we will *not* be sidetracked. We will *not* stop."

NOW THIS IS A PLAN I LIKE!

No problem. Sanballat and Tobiah pulled out Plan C. They did their homework. They sent some FBI agents to G.C.C. (Galilean Community College) and found out that Nehemiah had walked away from a full basketball scholarship to rebuild the wall. They knew athletics was important to him and could possibly be his weak spot.

"Nehemiah," Sanballat said. "We realize we've given you a hard time about rebuilding the wall. But the past is over, and we'd like to do our part to help bridge the gap between our cities."

Made sense. Nehemiah knew the tension between Jerusalem and the surrounding cities needed to be resolved.

"Nehemiah," Tobiah piped in. "We've decided to sponsor an inner-city basketball tournament. We'll coach the teams from our cities, and we want *you* to coach the Jerusalem team."

Nehemiah's interest was rising high. He knew he'd make a terrific coach. He was a natural.

"Of course," Sanballat said, "this means you'll need to take a little time off from the construction site to recruit your players, teach them strategy, and get them into shape."

"Tell you what," Tobiah said. "We'll give you six months to work with your team, and then we'll begin the tournament."

That sounded great! If there was one thing Nehemiah loved, it was sports. The sweat of competition and the thrill of victory raced through his imagination. His heart quickened. *I could take our men all the way to first place,* he thought. So that night he talked to the Lord about it.

"Father, this would be a great way to bridge the gap between the neighboring cities, and I know that's important to You."

"Yes, Nehemiah, that *is* important. But at this particular time, what's *more* important?"

"I guess rebuilding the wall."

"That's right."

"But God, this is such a *good* thing."

"Yes, it is. But what's the *better* thing?"

"Rebuilding the wall."

"Right."

DO TROUBLEMAKERS EVER STOP?

So the next morning, Nehemiah turned down the basket-ball challenge, forcing the two wicked governors to their final strategy: Plan D.

This time Sanballat and Tobiah forged a letter to Nehemiah from the king. The letter expressed gratitude and admiration for the work Nehemiah had done on the wall. It also stated that the government thought Nehemiah was an excellent role model for the youth of the nation. And because of Nehemiah's excellent leadership ability, the king was honoring him with a special seat in Congress. Of course, this meant that Nehemiah would have to take some time off to accept the award and fulfill some publicity obligations.

Nehemiah was ecstatic! He realized this would be a fantastic witness to all teens everywhere. Because of his new platform, people would certainly listen to him when he talked about the Lord.

That night, he talked with God about the situation.

"Lord, this is fantastic! Think of the witness I'll be."

"Yes, Nehemiah. A good witness is important. But at this particular time in your life, what's the *most* important?"

"Rebuilding the wall of righteousness that guards our land?"

"That's right."

But Lord, this is such a *good* thing!"

"Yes, being a witness in the public eye is good. But right now, what's the *best* thing?"

"Doing your will for my life. Rebuilding the wall of right-eousness."

"You're quick, Nehemiah."

Through discussing the matter with God, Nehemiah began to realize that the letter was a forgery, and that the two governors were secretly planning on killing him.

Nehemiah's Response

The next day Nehemiah sent a reply to Sanballat and Tobiah. Check out his response: "I am doing a great work! Why should I stop to come and visit with you?" (Nehemiah 6:3, TLB). In other words: *"What I am doing is the most important thing in the world, because I'm doing the will of God. Why should anything sidetrack me from accomplishing what my Father has called me to do?"*

In just fifty-two days after they had started, the construction crew completed the rebuilding of the wall around the entire city of Jerusalem. Wow! Less than two months—that's incredible! How did they do it?

They were consistent. Day after day, they placed brick upon brick. They refused to allow *anything* to sidetrack them from doing God's will.

Just as God commissioned Nehemiah to rebuild the wall of righteousness, He also commissions *you* to build a wall of righteousness. The place? Your life.

Nehemiah continued to complete the work God had called him to, even though it was clearly unpopular with unbelievers. Following God's job description for *your* life may not be applauded by unbelievers. Do you quit? No way! You continue building God's kingdom by doing what He instructs you to do.

Stuff You Don't Have to Pray About

Just what is this wall of righteousness? It's a strong, rock-solid relationship with Jesus Christ. And yes, He wants you to build one. No need to pray about it. He's already made it clear. *Wanted: Construction Workers . . . disciples who will invest time and commitment into building a strong, steady, solid wall of righteousness around their lives.*

You also don't have to pray about whether or not to lay aside the work you're doing for Christ when you receive flack from non-Christians. Keep on keepin' on!

STUFF YOU SHOULD PRAY ABOUT

Instead of praying about whether or not God wants you to build a righteous wall (or a strong relationship with Him), pray about:

1. Realizing that what you do is IMPORTANT. Nehemiah learned the importance to God of each individual. "I am doing a great work." What *you* do for God is important. It matters! You may think your role is small and goes unnoticed, but *anything* you do for Christ matters a great deal.

Your church needs help on clean-up day? Your contribution to the offering will make a difference? Your youth minister needs someone to call the visitors? What you do *matters*. Never think just because you're one person, your work won't help advance the kingdom. God needs individuals just like you.

Ammunition: 1 Thessalonians 1:7–8. According to this passage, what kind of impact can *you* have on those around you?

2. Asking for the strength to be consistent. Repeat after me: "I *will* build the wall of righteousness. I *will* stick it out. I *won't* allow myself to be sidetracked. I *am* going to see this thing through." Brick upon brick. Step by step. Keep following Jesus. THAT'S how growth happens.

Ammunition: 2 Corinthians 4:7–9. Memorize it. You'll be glad you did. (I promise.)

3. Continuing to do God's work in the midst of strife. The Apostle Paul was beaten, shipwrecked, and imprisoned. Did he take these inconveniences as a sign to call it quits? No, he remained consistent in completing the work God had given him to do.

Ammunition: Read Matthew 7:21. According to this Scripture, what's more important—talk or action? God calls us to do what's right, to continue His work in spite of the conflicts around us.

Father, I realize there's nothing more important in all the world than doing Your will. And I know that for right now, Your will is for me to build a strong wall of righteousness around my life.

Help me to be more consistent in my relationship with You. I get sidetracked so easily. So many people and activities compete for my attention. But the bottom line is, I don't *want* to be distracted from doing Your will. I WANT a strong relationship with You. Keep my feet on the right path and my eyes focused on You, so that when others make fun of me for continuing Your work, I will consistently carry on. Amen.

STUFF TO GROW ON #2

The Apostle Paul asks an interesting question in his letter to the Philippians: "Is there any such thing as Christians cheering each other up?" (2:1, TLB).

Take some time to cheer up some of the people in *your* life. Write an encouraging note expressing your appreciation to those you may take for granted:

- Your mom and dad
- A favorite school teacher
- The person who leads the music at your church
- A grandparent
- Your pastor
- Your brother(s)/sister(s)
- Four special friends
- An unrelated adult in your life who's involved in teaching you something (coach, employer, piano teacher, discipleship leader, gymnastics instructor, etc.)

- An aunt
- Sunday School teacher
- A cousin
- Someone you don't know personally, but who has made a positive impact on your life (a contemporary Christian artist, writer, missionary, evangelist, government official, etc.)
- An uncle
- Someone who probably doesn't get much encouragement (school bus driver, mailman, librarian, school cafeteria workers, etc.)

5

THE WORLD'S LARGEST BACKPACKING GROUP (PART 1)

They were like a huge youth group. They had waaaay over 300,000 kids. When they played "Capture the Flag," it was all-out war! And car washes? Well, let's just say the whole city got wet.

Their youth leader was Yo-Mo. Well, that's what the youth group called him. Everyone has a special nickname for their youth minister, right? And that was theirs. His real name was Moses, but Yo-Mo just fit him better.

Anyway, these teens (the world's largest backpacking group) had worked *forever* (OK, three months) to earn enough money to go on the world's longest backpacking trip. They'd had the car washes, spaghetti dinners, rock-a-thons, and had even tried selling M&Ms. (They couldn't sell 'em all, so they pawned the rest off on the senior pastor.)

Now they were arriving at their weekly youth meeting, and Yo-Mo, who was usually greeting kids and asking visitors to fill out address cards, had his head buried inside the youth bank account books instead.

"You've done it!" he screamed. "You've finally done it!" A few of the students looked sheepish and were heard murmuring among themselves, "I didn't think *anyone* saw us put those gold-fish in the baptistry. How'd he find out?"

Then Yo-Mo grabbed the mic and said, "I'm so proud of you guys! You've finally earned enough money for us to go on the world's longest backpacking trip."

ANNOUNCING THE DETAILS

Boy, were they excited! They shouted and clapped and screamed and were so loud that the adults (who were meeting in the sanctuary) complained about how much noise the youth were making again.

Yo-Mo didn't waste any time. He quickly grabbed his travel notes and gave his speech. "I've already mapped out the place for our adventure," he began. "We're going to the Promised Land. They have some great deals on milk and honey there, and it should only take us about forty days to backpack it.

(Well, some of you have heard this story before, and you know it actually took a little longer than forty days! But that's what happens when we get sidetracked from God's path. It takes us a lot longer than it would have if we'd just continued follow-ing His direction.)

He then passed out parent-permission forms, so no one could sue the church if something happened to a teen. And he continued with his instructions. "Since this is a backpacking trip, obviously that means we'll be carrying everything in our packs on our backs. So you know what that means, girls? No curling irons, electric rollers, or blow-dryers. Nobody bring *any-thing* extra."

"And guys . . . Well . . . ," he stopped. He was going to tell them the same thing. But he knew these guys. He knew they *never* brought too much stuff on trips. In fact when they went to youth camp or special retreats, they usually didn't even bring enough stuff—just a pair of jeans and a T-shirt. And if it got dirty? No prob. They just turned them inside out and kept wearing them!

"We'll meet here at the church tomorrow morning at 5:00 A.M.," Yo-Mo said. "And remember, it'll only take us forty days to get there . . . so we should be back at the church by . . . ," and he told the teens the specific day and time they'd be returning. "So, tell your parents to just be here waiting for you," he said. "Because I don't want to wait for 300,000 of you to call your parents once we get back to the church, OK?"

Will it Ever End?

Now I don't know about the teens in *your* youth group, but the kids in Yo-Mo's group weren't very good travelers. They got antsy before the buses even arrived at the spot they were going to backpack from. They wanted to stop at every McDonald's they passed. They screamed stuff from the back of the buses. Annoying stuff such as: "How many more miles?" and "When're we gonna get there?"

And once they actually started backpacking, their questions turned accusatory: "Hey! Yo-Mo, you *said* the trip would last forty days. It's been four-and-a-half *years!*" And even derogatory remarks, "Yo-Mo! Where'd you get your compass? Out of a Cracker Jacks box?"

Finally, after thirteen years, some of the guys really let him have it. "Yo-Mo! We gave up basketball camp for this! When are we gettin' there, man?"

And after twenty-five years, the girls started in. "Oh, I'm soooo shuuure. It's like, c'mon Yo-Mo. I mean, we ran outta Flex Shampoo like twenty-four years ago. Gag! So when are we gonna get there, huh?"

After thirty-seven years, a kid from the very back of the group raised his hand. "Um, Mr. Yo-Mo? Do you have a cell phone? I, uh, really oughta call my parents. They've been waiting for me at the church for thirty-seven years now. I mean, you said we'd be back around . . ."

REST STOP

Finally, Yo-Mo decided to stop at an oasis. Everyone took off their packs and sat down to rest while he climbed a mountain. (You'd probably want to stretch *your* legs, too, if you'd been backpacking for forty years with 300,000 teens.)

When Moses reached the top of the mountain, the Lord began speaking. "Mo, squint your eyes a little. See way over there in the distance?"

Yo squinted. "Yeah. I see it!"

"Well, that's the Promised Land," the Lord said.

"Wow!" Mo exclaimed. "That's it? That's what we've been trying to find for the past forty years?"

"That's it."

"Cool!"

"And now that you've seen it, it's time for you to die."

What?

Over forty years of leading his youth group, and now he has to die? Without even getting to go *inside?*

That's right. You see, a little earlier, Mo had compromised (made excuses for things that were really wrong, but said it was OK), so God was withholding some of His blessings.

CHANGES IN LEADERSHIP

Meanwhile, the youth group had turned into a mumbling, grumbling bunch of complainers. "Where *is* he?" someone asked. "Can we go ahead and eat, or do we have to wait on him?"

But when a messenger sent to find Yo-Mo returned with the sad news that their leader had died, the youth group changed their tune. They moaned, cried, refused to eat, and didn't sleep very well.

"Now what are we going to do," they asked. "We've left everything to enter the Promised Land, and now we have no leader!"

Well, God never ever *ever* asks us to do something (or leads us somewhere) without providing everything we need to get the job done. He *always* meets our needs. And God had already been working. He already had His hand of direction on a young man in their very own youth group. Maybe you've heard of him—his name was Joshua.

Josh was a solid, godly young man. He didn't compromise. Didn't buckle when the pressure began to mount. Didn't bend when the tension started to rise. He just walked straight ahead and consistently obeyed the Lord.

He took Mo's maps and called the youth group together. "I've studied the travel plans," he said. "And we're really not far from the Promised Land at all." (Everyone cheered.) "But there is this big city in the way. It's Jericho. And it's a very wicked city. So we're going to have to go through it and conquer it before we can enter the Promised Land."

(Back in the days before Christ died for our sins, the way God abolished evil was to destroy it. That's why the guys in the Old Testament were always killing each other. It was the only plan at the time to clean everything up. Sure am glad Jesus came, aren't you?)

"Tell you what," Josh continued. "You've all been through a rough time. Let's just set up camp right here (they were on the shores of the Jordan River) and take a few days off. That'll give me a chance to send our FBI undercover agents inside the city of Jericho to see where everything is."

Sounded good. So while the agents crossed the river and headed toward the large city, the world's largest backpacking group set up the volleyball nets, got out the jet skis, and started partying.

Just How Big Is Big?

As soon as Josh's agents crossed the Jordan River, they were face to face with the largest wall they'd ever seen. It was huge—MASSIVE. And it surrounded the city of Jericho. But, hey, God always provides. (We talked about that a little earlier, remember?) And the gates to the city just happened to be open, so Josh's FBI agents meandered right through. One guy pulled out his Sony Camcorder and started taking movies so Joshua could see where everything was.

There was the city square. And off to the right was Jericho High School. And about five blocks away was Jericho Middle School. Across the street, he noticed Jericho Swim and Fitness. And up closer on the left were some really cool split-level condos.

Another guy took out his Polaroid and began snapping pics of other things. While they were busy looking like tourists (but actually *doing* important things), some of the king's employees were taking a coffee break and happened to see the spies.

They rushed back to the king and told him about the strangers with the cameras. "Hmmph," the king said. "Betcha they're part of that world's largest backpacking group. They're the ones who've been tramping around in the desert for about forty years. I think they're headed for the Promised Land, which probably means they'll try to conquer *us* before they get there."

UH-OH!

"Well, what should we do, O, Wise One?" one of the employees asked. ("O, Wise One?" C'mon! Who really talks like that? He was always trying to get on the king's good side.)

"We're going to lock the gates to the city so anyone who's not a citizen won't be able to get in! And if we see anyone trying to get in or out, we'll kill him on the spot."

Wow! Major plan of destruction. But remember, God always provides. The king's employees weren't the only ones watching those FBI agents. There was a woman named Rahab (sound like anyone you've shared a locker with? Don't you love these Old Testament names?) who was standing on the balcony of her condo wringing out her wet laundry. (True story.)

She wanted to help these men of God, and she'd also over-heard the conversation of the king's employees. So while the agents were still taking pictures, she tried to catch their attention.

"Psssst."

Click. Click.

"Pssssst."

Click. "Hey, Eric! Stand over there by that fountain and act like you're gonna fall in. THAT'LL make a great shot."

"Psssssst."

• "Oooooh, yeah. And get one of me next to this statue."

"Pssssssst."

"Hey! Betcha we could make a postcard outta *that* one!"

"Psssssssst!"

"Ryan, did you hear something?"

"No, don't think so."

"Pssssssssst!"

"Wait a minute. Maybe I did."

"Psssssssssst!"

"Yeah. What *was* that?"

"PSSSSSSSSSSSSSTTTTTTT!!!"

"Eric, there's a lady up there making faces at us!"

"No, I think she's doing her laundry."

"What's she want?"

"Beats me. Ask her."

"Uh . . . ma'am. Are you talking to *us*?" (Duh!)

"Yeah, but I can't talk very loudly because I don't want anyone to hear me."

"That's okay. Ryan's pretty good at reading lips and watching hand signals. Sharp guy this Ryan."

"The king's gonna kill you! If you want . . . you can climb up here and hide underneath my dirty laundry."

Sounded like a plan. After all they had no other options! So they hid on her balcony until nightfall.

IF IT'S NOT ONE THING, IT'S ANOTHER

Rahab was a talented woman—I guess she used to work for the rodeo or something—because as soon as the sun set, she grabbed a rope, made a lasso and tossed it over the wall. The agents climbed down the rope over the wall and headed back to Joshua's party.

"You're not gonna believe it," Ryan gasped.

"It's HUGE!" Eric added. "And we have pictures and videos to prove it."

"We almost got killed!" Ryan said.

"Yeah, and there's absolutely no way we could ever conquer the city," added Eric. "It's too big and there are too many people. Probably six times our size!"

"But not only that," said Ryan, "there's this MASSIVE wall that surrounds the entire city! We'll never get inside. They have a special warrant issued for all non-citizens to be killed. We'd never get over the wall!"

"Someone hand these boys a Coke," Josh said, keeping his cool. "I think you guys have forgotten something."

Ryan quickly checked his battery pack. "Nope. All here."

"Our *theme*," Josh said. "You've forgotten our theme."

"What's that?" Eric asked.

"The fact that God always provides! Even Rahab was part of God's provision. Guys, listen to me! He would never ever EVER ask us to do something (or lead us somewhere) without providing everything we need. Now remember that! In fact, *memorize* it. Because we *are* going to the Promised Land. And we're going through Jericho!"

OKAY, BUT . . .

Plans were made to head out the following morning, but by dawn the Jordan River was flooded. As in overflowing. We're talking tidal wave. Joshua halted his group. "Let's just spend a few days in prayer and wait on the Lord."

So they waited. And waited. And waited. Finally a couple of weeks passed. The river was still overflowing. It looked like they would drown if they even tried to cross. Joshua continued to seek the Lord. And as he did, God spoke back.

"Joshua, I have commanded that you cross this river, conquer Jericho, and enter the Promised Land. What are you waiting on?"

"The river, Lord. It's flooded. It's overflowing! How can we cross?"

"Trust Me. I've already told you to cross."

"But, Lord, are You sure we're supposed to cross *right now?* I mean, we don't mind waiting," Josh said.

"You don't need to spend time praying about things I've already made clear, Joshua. There may be some battles in life you won't win, but I have already promised THIS is one you *will* win! I've already made Myself clear: Cross the river, conquer Jericho, enter the Promised Land. No need to continue praying about it. Simply step out in faith believing that I will do what I have said."

So Josh gathered the world's largest backpacking group together and lined them up. Row after row after row. Over 300,000 of them. And I imagine his instructions went something like this:

"Okay, gang, we're crossing. I know. I know. I know. The Jordan River is still flooded. I realize that. But I also have faith that the God who calls us to cross will somehow provide a way. I mean, that's our *theme*, right? Let's join hands and walk together."

So they began. Ryan's hand was pretty sweaty, but he clung to his brother Eric. And Eric clung to Joshua. And Joshua clung to Geoff. And Geoff clung to Woodie. And Woodie clung to Cheryl. And Cheryl clung to Michelle. And on and on and on it went—all holding hands and walking toward this huge powerful body of roaring, terrifying fifteen-foot waves.

You know what happened, don't you? Their feet touched the water and God split the river! (If Eric would've been thinking, he could've grabbed the Sony Camcorder and videoed the whole thing for us. But he was so shocked it was all he could do to keep putting one foot in front of the other while his mouth hung open.) Over 300,000 people walked across on dry land.

WHAT A STRATEGY!

As soon as they crossed the Jordan River, they were up against the largest wall they'd ever seen in their lives. But everyone remained calm. Josh had already gone over the game plan. He'd already rehearsed the instructions. They knew exactly what to do.

They reached behind their heads and untied their backpacks. (Even though Yo-Mo had specifically said NOT to bring anything extra—everyone had. It just so happened that forty years earlier, they were all members of the Egyptian Junior and Senior High School marching band.) They pulled out their horns, tubas, flutes, and other music makers and lined up. After tuning up, they marched around the great wall playing "Oh, When the Saints Go Marching In."

And the people inside the city of Jericho stopped. "Oh, when the saints," someone sang. "Go marching in," someone hummed. "Oh, when the saints go marching in," a soprano belted.

"Hey! I know that song."

"Where's that music coming from?"

"Did our city decide to pipe in music for us?"

"That's sooo special!"

And the next day at the same time, the world's largest backpacking group marched around the wall again and played the same tune. And the next day. And the *next*. And the *next*. Until finally at the end of the week, the people inside the city of Jericho were sick and tired of the same old music.

"Hey, can't you play anything else besides 'The Saints'?" someone yelled.

"Yeah, we're SICK of that song!"

"How 'bout a C-scale or a minor chord or one of those augmented things—SOMETHING!"

"We will not play that kind of music," Josh said to his group. "In fact, since this is the seventh day, just for spite, let's play our theme song SEVEN times. Ha! That'll get 'em!"

So they adjusted their instruments and began marching. But this time, as a grand finale at the end of the seventh rendition, they threw their instruments on the ground. They stood tall with their shoulders back and screamed as loudly as they could: "JOE!"

The people inside Jericho's walls stopped. *Joe?* Men who were coming out of the bank and placing money in their wallets stopped. *Joe?*

Women who were pushing babies in strollers down sidewalks stopped. *Joe?*

Adults who were coming out of grocery stores with bags in their arms stopped. *Joe?*

Teachers who were lecturing and writing notes on chalkboards stopped. *Joe?*

And students who were listening and taking notes, stopped. Joe? Joe! *Joe?*

Finally, the entire city dumbfounded, stood to their feet and in unison cried out, "JOE? JOE WHO?"

Over 300,000 on the other side screamed back: *Joe Mama!*

Joe Mama is a wimp! Joe Mama wears army boots. Joe Mama Joe Mama! Joe MAMA!

There was so much noise, the walls began to shake. The ground trembled, and only minutes later, the entire wall completely collapsed.

The world's largest backpacking group wasted no time. They rushed inside wielding weapons, and with Roman candles for special effect. The people of Jericho were in such a state of shock and confusion, they were not only defeated but slaughtered on the spot! God had provided victory—even when the children of Israel couldn't see where it came from or how it came about.

STUFF YOU DON'T HAVE TO PRAY ABOUT

As Christians, God calls us to live a "step above" the rest of the world. He wants *you* to be **set apart.** That means trusting Him when nothing makes sense. There is specific purpose in everything He asks us to do.

Even when we don't know where the resources will come from, God will provide. He's committed to meeting our needs. He will NOT ask us to do something and then frustrate us by not equipping us with everything we need to accomplish the task.

When we face a desert experience, we don't have to beg God to meet our needs. Our responsibility? Simply make our needs known and trust Him to provide.

One way He meets our needs is through others within the body of Christ. He wants us to reach out and be His hands to those around us. Besides having faith that He will directly meet our individual needs, He also wants to use US to help provide for others in the church.

STUFF YOU SHOULD PRAY ABOUT

Instead of begging God to meet your needs, spend time praying for:

1. A future of faith. Ask God to increase your trust in His promise to take care of you. He is committed to meeting your needs even when you can't see where the resources will come from.

Ammunition: 2 Kings 4:1–7. What happened when the widow filled her pots and pans? This shows us that God's provision is as large as our faith. How can you exercise your faith this week? God not only wants to meet our needs right now—He's also committed to providing for us in the future. Therefore, pray for a growing faith to increase daily.

2. A lifestyle reflective of faith. Anyone can talk about faith. And it's easy to claim we have it. But the real test comes in whether or not we echo our trust in God by the way we live. Pray that Christ will help you act and react in accordance with a strong faith in Him.

Ammunition: 2 Kings 13:4–6. What did Jehoahaz pray for God to help him with? And when God provided for him, what was his reaction? Did his lifestyle reflect his trust in the Creator? When God provides for you, how can your life reflect your continued trust in Him?

3. A powerful, positive faith. Check out Psalm 11:1–4. As God meets the needs of the psalmist, what is his attitude? Trusting God to meet our needs is linked to optimism. When things don't seem to be going your way, how can you maintain a positive attitude? Can you see how establishing a positive daily trust in the Lord can affect your entire lifestyle?

4. The desire to allow God to work through YOU to be part of His provision for others. How did the world's largest backpacking group cross the Jordan River? By holding hands and walking together. You see, God promises that there's *nothing* we'll face that will be too strong for us to handle—if we're walking together. That's what the body of Christ is all about.

It's about patting someone on the shoulder and saying, "Good job!" Or looking a friend in the eye and saying, "Jamie, I sense that you're going through a tough time right now. Can I treat you to a Coke?" It's walking the second mile. Mailing a note of encouragement to someone. Making a phone call. Giving a hug.

Ammunition: John 13:34–35. What is our proof that we belong to Christ? As you reach out to someone this week, trust God to work through you to meet the needs of another person.

Lord, I admit that many times I can't see how You're going to meet my needs. But I know—based on Your Word—that You WILL provide. Teach me how to multiply my faith. I want it to effect every area of my life—my attitudes, the way I react to those around me, and my spiritual growth. Help me to realize that I don't have to beg You to come through for me. Remind me that even when I'm in the middle of a confusing situation, You're already working on the solution. Thank You, Lord. In Your name I pray, Amen.

6

THE WORLD'S LARGEST BACKPACKING GROUP (PART 2)

Now that the children of Israel had taken over the city of Jericho, Joshua lost no time. He grabbed the microphone at city square and announced the continuing plan of action. "Glory be to God!" he cried, "for giving us the strength to defeat a city six times our size. Now listen carefully to the following instructions. I want everyone to go into every condo, home, and apartment and destroy everything except anything that's valuable."

"Like what?" Todd asked. (It had been so long since any of them had even seen valuable stuff, they were a little confused. That's what wandering around in the desert for forty years can do to you.)

"Jewelry," Josh said. "Bring all the jewelry out here—along with any valuable metals—you know, turquoise, gold, silver, copper. We'll melt it all down and use it to build the temple once we get to the Promised Land. Bring the valuable stuff out to city square, destroy the rest—and NO ONE KEEP ANYTHING FOR HIMSELF!"

Pretty clear. Josh gave the signal and away they went. All of them. Following his orders. Obeying the instructions. Well . . . not exactly. There was this one guy. (There's always *one* in every crowd, isn't there?)

SUCH A SMALL THING

His name was Acorn. (Well, almost. People probably *called* him that when they made fun of him. His real name was Achan. Not much better, huh?)

Acorn went into a condo, cleaned it out completely, and just happened to notice a bathrobe. (Read the story for yourself in the seventh chapter of Joshua.) And even though he remembered Josh specifically saying no one could keep anything, Acorn thought to himself, *Hey, it's just a bathrobe. It's not like it's valuable or anything.* And besides . . . no one was watching. *I am so tired of these old gym shorts. I deserve a new bathrobe.* So he TOOK the garment, folded it up, wrapped his tunic around it, and went to the next home.

Again, he cleaned it out completely, but his eyes fell on a small gold bar—maybe three inches long. And even though he could hear Joshua's words echoing in his mind, Acorn couldn't help but think, *It's so small. What's one gold bar?* And no one was around. Everyone else was busy with their own jobs. So he TOOK the gold bar, stuck it in his pocket, and went to a nearby apartment.

He did a great job cleaning it out, but as he did, he couldn't help but see a small silver coin—about the size of two quarters.

And yes, he remembered the words of his leader, but different thoughts ran through his mind: *It's just a silver coin. I mean, it's been forty years since I've had an allowance. I DESERVE this little bit of money. I'm working hard, here!* And you gotta remember, no one was looking. *It's not like they NEED this small coin,* he thought. And true, it really wouldn't be missed. People were hauling large sections of golden walls and pieces of solid silver, turquoise, and other metals. One small coin really wasn't going to matter in the grand scheme of things.

So he took the silver coin and went back to his personal tent, dug a hole in the ground and placed the coins in the pocket of the bathrobe, folded the robe, buried it, placed his cot on top of the dirt and probably put his stereo on top of that.

It was smooth. No one nearby. Nothing would be missed.

PARTY TIME!

That night, the world's largest backpacking group celebrated their victory . . . big-time. They had been eating manna (Wonder Bread-like stuff that God had sent from heaven) and quail meat for forty years. But this night they grilled hot dogs over a blazing campfire, roasted marshmallows, and even made s'mores.

They were on cloud nine, and so was their leader. "God has been faithful," Josh reminded them. "We're so close to the Promised Land, that we will be there tomorrow night!" Everyone screamed and clapped and a few guys in the back stuck their fingers in their mouths and whistled real loud.

"According to the map," Josh said, "there's one more city that stands between us and the Promised Land. It's a peanut-sized city. We're talking teeny-tiny. In fact, we don't even need to send our entire army. I'll have our top fighters leave tomorrow morning to conquer it and they'll be done in just a couple of hours. Then they'll come back and get us around noon, and we'll be in our dream land tomorrow evening in time for supper!"

Sounded pretty good. Can you even imagine camping out for forty years?

The next morning, the top fighters from the world's largest backpacking group left to conquer the city of Ai. But just before noon, a messenger came back to camp. He explained to Joshua that every man had been killed in battle.

"What?" Josh cried. "That can't be true! Ai is such a small city."

The Bible tells us he was so distraught, he threw himself on the ground, tore his clothes, and cried out to his heavenly Father. I imagine his prayer went something like this: "God, I don't understand. You've been so faithful until now. You've split the Jordan River, parted the Red Sea, given us water from rocks, turned a snake into a stick, led us with a pillar of light in the darkness, given us bread from heaven, quail meat, and just gave us victory over a city SIX TIMES our size!

"Now that we're this close to the Promised Land, You choose to walk away and leave us? How can this be? Why would You bring us this far just to tease us? *I don't understand!* Is this some kind of sick joke? Are You just gonna leave us out here to die?"

God listened to Joshua's prayer. And He also responded. In fact, His response was such a classic, that Josh memorized it, then wrote it down.

"I cannot honor a group of people who choose to compromise."

Ooooh.

WHAT A NIGHTMARE!

As soon as Joshua heard those words, he KNEW someone had rationalized the instructions. Someone had TAKEN something that didn't belong to him.

So he gathered his search party and told them to go into every person's tent, dig through everyone's belongings, and find the stolen property.

They did. And they came up empty-handed. Acorn didn't even bat an eye. Why should he? No one had seen him, and he'd buried his stolen treasures underneath his cot. No one would ever think to dig a hole in the floor of his tent.

But Joshua wouldn't give up. (He never buckled under pressure, remember?) So the search party went back again. And again they came up empty-handed.

But Joshua *still* didn't quit. He sent his men back *again*. They came to Acorn's tent. Searched it inside and out. No one found a thing. They left.

Except for one man. He stopped in the doorway of the tent, spun around, and folded his arms. His eyes darted from side to side. *What is it?* he thought. *What's this eerie feeling I have? Ahh, I don't know. I'm just so tired of searching everything and coming up empty-handed.*

He wandered back inside the tent and threw everything off the walls. Then he kicked the cot out the door and took the pillow and smashed it against his knees until the feathers flew out. Then, standing where the cot had been, he folded his arms again and began kicking the dirt underneath his feet while scanning the tent.

And you guessed it. As he stood and kicked, you know what he saw. The corner of a colored bathrobe. And as he leaned over to pick it up, a silver coin and a gold bar fell out of the pocket.

Acorn was brought to the center of the camp and burned alive.

Wow! What started as a fun story about an exciting youth group, suddenly turned into a nightmare. All because one guy *compromised*.

So It All Comes Down To...

You see, there are some things that change. The weather. The price of a hamburger. History. Fashion. And then there are things *you* change: your mind, your socks (I hope!), your feelings, your grades.

But there are some things that NEVER change. And those things are God's laws. They don't rotate, alter, shift, or evolve. They're constant. Solid. Concrete. They will always be that way.

When we compromise God's standards, we're sinning. *Sin* is a word we don't hear a lot about anymore. The world says, "It's not *sin*, it's just doing your own thing." But when God says "no," and you say "yes," it's *sin*.

We live in a gray world. In other words, right and wrong have fused together to create "whatever's right for the moment." And for Acorn, it seemed "right at the moment" to take some gold, silver, and a bathrobe.

It's wrong to steal. It's wrong to sin. It always *has* been and it always *will* be. Maybe for you the issue isn't stealing . . . maybe it's going too far with your boy- or girlfriend. Or maybe it's the language that you use or the movies you're watching or _____ (you fill in the blank). But the bottom line is, if you're rationalizing (making excuses for something that's really wrong and convincing yourself it's OK), then you're living in sin.

"So how much does it cost to live in sin?" Well, it costs a lot. The Bible says the cost is death (Romans 6:23). The cost was death when Acorn lived, the cost is death today, and the cost will still be death one thousand years from now. That's not changing. And that's bad news.

But there's more. Here's the *good* news! The Bible also says that God will forgive for the asking (1 John 1:9).

STUFF YOU DON'T HAVE TO PRAY ABOUT

When you do something the world says is permissible, but it lowers your standards or hinders your relationship with Christ, you're *compromising* to keep pace with those around you. God calls you to keep in step with Him.

ANYTHING that compromises where you stand with God is wrong. You don't even need to spend time praying about it. For Acorn, it was taking something that didn't belong to him. It would have been a waste of time for him to pray, "Lord, You know I'm broke and need a little extra money. Thanks for helping me find this gold and silver. And thanks for no one seeing me take it. Now, don't let anyone find my treasures while I bury them, okay?"

I know. I know. You're thinking, *That's stupid. Who'd ever pray a prayer like that?* Well, don't we do the same thing when we drive too fast? *Lord, You know I don't want to be late for church, so I'm going to have to speed. Don't let me get stopped.*

Or possibly when you're watching something you shouldn't? *Lord, don't let Mom and Dad come home till this is over.*

You get the picture. No need to pray about anything you have to rationalize. Why? Because God's already made it clear.

Stuff You Should Pray About

Instead of spending your time praying about things that will compromise your walk with God, pray for:

1. Wisdom to know the difference. Maybe you're not sure if this specific thing will compromise your relationship with Him or not. Seek His wisdom. He's more than ready to give you solid direction when you ask.

Ammunition: James 1:5–8. In what specific way does this passage encourage you to pray? Check out Proverbs 3:13–15. How important is wisdom? And what does Proverbs 3:16–18 tell you about wisdom? Continue reading—Proverbs 3:19–20. What role did wisdom have in the creation of the earth? And look at Psalm 119:1–3. What do these verses have to say about compromise?

2. Discernment. Discernment is honed wisdom. It allows you to be more than just "generally wise." Discernment helps you assess specific situations and know from the inside out whether or not it's right.

Ammunition: For clues about how important discernment is, read Proverbs 3:21–26. According to these verses, what will discernment help you to do?

3. Knowledge. If you *are* rationalizing something and it's not right in God's eyes, you want to know about it. So pray for that knowledge. That's why daily devotions (time spent with God in prayer and reading the Bible) are so important—it gives you a chance to ask God if there's anything in your life that's not right. Then it's His responsibility to help you know what it is. And when He brings it to your mind (when you have *knowledge* of it), seek His forgiveness and commit it to Him. So go ahead. Let Him look under your cot. Anything there that's displeasing to Him?

Ammunition: Psalm 139:23–24. How does God's Spirit work like a spotlight in your life? How can implementing this Scripture affect your life?

> Lord, sometimes I move so fast, I forget to stop and think about if what I'm doing is really okay in Your sight. I hurry to keep up with my friends . . . when I should be hurrying to keep myself saturated in Your Word.
>
> I don't want to compromise, Father. My *desire* is to live a life that's pleasing to You. I need Your discernment, Your wisdom, and Your strength. Help me to discipline myself daily to establishing those attributes in my life. Help me to work at them—practice them—until they become part of my lifestyle. I want to live with integrity, never compromising. Never rationalizing.
>
> Help me to be like Joshua, standing strong when the pressure rises. I don't want to buckle when I feel the tension. But "as for me and my house . . . I WILL serve the Lord." Amen.

STUFF TO GROW ON #3

Use the following verses from the Old Testament as spiritual "vitamins." Copy them on index cards and place them in key areas (on your light switch, dresser, dashboard, inside your locker, bedpost, mirror, etc.) and refer to them throughout the day to keep your mind focused on the right stuff.

Lord, when doubts fill my mind, when my heart is in turmoil, quiet me and give me renewed hope and cheer (Psalm 94:19, TLB).

Be strong and courageous. Do not be afraid or terrified because of them, for the LORD your God goes with you; he will never leave you nor forsake you (Deuteronomy 31:6, NIV).

Because of the LORD's great love we are not consumed, for his compassions never fail. They are new every morning; great is your faithfulness (Lamentations 3:22–23, NIV).

Even though the fig trees are all destroyed, and there is neither blossom left nor fruit, and though the olive crops all fail, and the fields lie barren; even if the flocks die in the fields and the cattle barns are empty, yet I will rejoice in the Lord; I will be happy in the God of my salvation (Habakkuk 3:17–18, TLB).

But they that wait upon the Lord shall renew their strength. They shall mount up with wings like eagles; they shall run and not be weary; they shall walk and not faint (Isaiah 40:31, TLB).

Search the Book of the Lord and see all that he will do; not one detail will he miss (Isaiah 34:16, TLB).

7

DO I HAVETA LOVE WILLIAM?

When I was a high school teacher, I had a student in my class who sat near the back of the room and made animal noises all hour. William didn't have many friends (would you want to sit next to someone who sounded like he was emitting a moose mating signal?), and he was dying for attention. But I didn't want to love him.

When I was a youth minister, there was a girl in our group who smelled. Always. And her hair was oily. *Very oily.* And when we took trips, none of the kids wanted to sit next to her on the bus. And on retreats? No one wanted to bunk with Elizabeth. She was dying for friends. But I didn't want to love her.

When I started speaking and traveling a lot, I noticed there was usually one kid who just latched on to me. This one kid would usually run to the cafeteria to sit with me, seek me out during free time, and hang onto my arm or hand as I walked from area to area. And this one kid never had any friends (why else would a teen purposely hang out with the speaker?), needed some deodorant, hadn't brushed his teeth, and was picked on by everyone else. This one kid was always dying to be loved. But I didn't want to love him.

65

Then there was this adult. She didn't always say or do the right things. She was impulsive and spontaneous—and many times she would *do* before she *thought*. She was impatient with people and held unreal expectations of others. Though she had friends, she was still dying to be loved—intimately.

And you know what? Even though she was far from perfect, Someone loved her anyway. And not just a little bit. He loved her as if she were the only one in all the world to love. He treated her like a queen—He even *died for* her. And because JESUS cared enough to love ME (and I'm still impulsive), I in turn must love others.

Not just when it's convenient and easy. Not just when they smell good and look great. Not just the popular people and the funny, outgoing, creative ones. It means if I'm going to call myself a *disciple*, I will love others, period. William. Elizabeth. The lonely kid at camp.

IT ALL COMES DOWN TO...

Years ago, I heard a story I've never forgotten. Chad was in the fourth grade. He was exceptionally small for his age and was never chosen for teams at recess—and during P.E. class when everyone had to be selected, he was always picked last.

Chad was shy. It was hard for him to talk to others—and he never knew what to say—so he just kept to himself.

He walked the one-half mile to school every day. And every morning, his mom would stand on the inside of the screen door and watch him leave till she couldn't see him any longer. Every afternoon, around 3:00 P.M., she'd stand at the window by the kitchen sink and watch a group of fourth-grade boys laughing and kicking rocks on their way home. And about a block behind them, walked Chad. Alone.

One day he came home excited and announced, "Mom, Valentine's Day is coming soon. And I want to make valentines for every kid in my class. Will you take me to the store so I can get all the stuff?"

Her heart sank. She knew her son. He threw his whole self into everything he did. She didn't want him to put a lot of time and energy into something that he wouldn't get back. But she also didn't want to rob him of this new-found excitement. So she agreed.

A Mission To Accomplish

After dinner Chad broke into his piggy bank, and they went to the store. He bought everything needed to make big, beautiful, homemade valentines—glitter, bright red construction paper, ribbons, white cardboard, brand-new crayons, markers, and stencils.

Every day after school, Chad passed right by the television, went straight to his room, and worked on the valentines. Some nights his mom could hardly even get him to the dinner table. She'd never seen her son so excited before.

After two weeks, he had finally completed his works of art. "Look at 'em, Mom! Aren't they great?" They were *glorious*. Beautiful in every sense of the word. Thirty-three bright red, homemade valentines sat on his dresser that night. He dreamed of giving them away the next morning.

When he woke, his mom helped him carefully wrap the hearts in a big box, then taped it closed in case he dropped them on the way to school in his excitement and hurry.

As she watched her son leave with the box tucked under his arm, she noted that he walked with confidence. And for good reason—he had worked hard for what he carried. But her heart sank. For she was afraid that no one would remember Chad when passing out valentines to each other.

She decided to make cookies that afternoon, and timed it so they'd just be coming out of the oven when he got home. *That'll take the sting out of his day*, she thought. Warm, gooey, chocolate chip cookies—his favorite.

Quarter of three rolled around, and she placed the cookies in the oven, then paced the floor. At 2:58 she pulled them out and placed them on the counter. At 3:00 she looked out the kitchen window and saw several fourth-grade boys laughing and bragging about their valentines. Their hands were full of little notes and cards of affirmation.

AND THEN THERE'S CHAD

And about a block behind, walked Chad. Alone. She squinted to see what he held in his hands. Books. Probably homework. His lunch pail. Any valentines? Still couldn't tell. But she did notice he was walking faster than usual. *He's probably about to cry*, she thought. *And he doesn't want anyone to see him. I'll hold the door open for him so he can get in faster.*

She walked to the front door just as he sailed past her screaming, "Mom!"

He ran into the kitchen and passed right by the warm, gooey, chocolate chip cookies and spun around. It was then she saw it. One valentine. Crumpled in his little sweaty hand. It was a dittoed valentine from the teacher. Same thing for every student. Nothing special. She reached out to grab him in her arms, when he started screaming again.

"Mom! There were exactly thirty-three kids in my class. And I made exactly thirty-three valentines. I put a homemade valentine in every single bag. I didn't forget anyone, Mom! I gave *each kid* a Valentine, and I didn't drop 'em or smash 'em. They were beautiful, Mom. And I had exactly enough for everyone. I didn't forget, Mom. I didn't forget *one single kid!* Isn't that great?"

And she started to cry. Not because her son hadn't received any valentines. But because Chad was so focused on loving others, he hadn't even noticed when he wasn't loved in return.

GOTTA SHOW THE WORLD

That's not a bad idea, is it? Giving our hearts away. Isn't that exactly what Jesus did for each of us? And it's comforting to know that He never asks us to do anything He hasn't done first.

In other words, when our Father commands us to reach out to those who are tough to love (the Williams and Elizabeths), He Himself enables us to do that by filling us with His love. *That's how Christians can truly love and make a difference.* And not just on Valentine's Day . . . but every day of the year. And not just when we're loved *back,* but even when we're overlooked or treated wrongly.

That's why I baked bread for my grouchy, hard-to-love next-door neighbor. She's *never* happy and complains about everything. And when she complained about my dog, I was furious. I wanted to yell at her. Instead, I took her some homemade bread.

And when she yelled at me for parking my car in the street instead of in my driveway, I wanted to send my dog over on an attack mission. Instead, I delivered her mail that was accidentally sent to me.

And when a new employee with a loud voice was given an office close to mine, I wanted to bang on the wall between our offices and say, "Hey! Quit talking so loud. I'm trying to write in here." And when I could hear her obnoxious laugh clear down the hallway, I wanted to scream, "Put a cork in it!" Instead, I invited her out to lunch. Got to know her. Found out she was struggling. Needed a friend. Felt insecure about her new position.

How will the world know we're Christians? By toting our new leatherbound Student Bibles? (Hardly.) By wearing a cool gold-plated cross around our neck? By quoting Scripture? (Satan did that.)

They'll know we are Christians by our *love.* And here's the hard part. Ready? They'll know we are Christians *not* by our love for God. That's the simple part. It's easy to love GOD. They'll know we are Christians by *our love for EACH OTHER!* (Oooh, that's tough!)

It's a lot easier for me to love *God* than for me to love *you.* That's where our true colors show. The mark of a mature disciple is his love for those around him.

Stuff You Don't Have to Pray About

Jeremy is saying unkind things about you behind your back. Should you love him? Yep. You don't even have to pray about it. Seems like Mrs. Thompson always picks on you during class. Should you love her? You bet! Don't even spend time praying about it. God has already made this "loving thing" explicitly clear . . . with His life.

Stuff You Should Pray About

Loving others is hard work. It requires conscious action. So pray specifically for:

1. Insight for avoiding arguments. Yeah, it's sometimes challenging to get into a heated argument, but remember, God is not calling you to win quarrels; He's calling you to LOVE OTHERS.

Ammunition: Soak up 1 Thessalonians 5:13 and Ephesians 4:31–32. What do these passages have to say about quarreling? What should we do instead of argue?

2. Strength to love others. Even when it's the last thing you want to do, God still calls you to love. Obviously, you can't do this in your own strength, so pray for His.

Ammunition: Check out Colossians 1:11. What will Christ's strength enable you to do?

3. A deep, growing love for others. Since Jesus displayed intimate love for us when He gave His life, we should also seek to love others beyond a surface, half-hearted commitment. Want others to see Christ's love in you? Then develop a deep, solid, genuine love for others.

Ammunition: Philippians 1:9–11. According to this passage, love and spiritual growth go together. What does the Apostle

Paul say will happen as we learn to love? Look at 1 Thessalonians 3:12–13. What's the reward for a growing love?

4. A LIFESTYLE of love. Yes, love is action. It's something you *do*. But it's also something you are. It's how you *be*. In other words, God wants His love to become more than reacting. He wants it to flow through your veins. To move you forward. To become your lifestyle.

Ammunition: 1 Corinthians 13 (the love chapter):

If I speak with human eloquence and angelic ecstasy but don't love, I'm nothing but the creaking of a rusty gate.

If I speak God's Word with power, revealing all his mysteries and making everything plain as day, and if I have faith that says to a mountain, "Jump," and it jumps, but I don't love, I'm nothing.

If I give everything I own to the poor and even go to the stake to be burned as a martyr, but I don't love, I've gotten nowhere. So, no matter what I say, what I believe, and what I do, I'm bankrupt without love.

Love never gives up.
Love cares more for others than for self.
Love doesn't want what it doesn't have.
Love doesn't strut,
Doesn't have a swelled head,
Doesn't force itself on others,
Isn't always "me first,"
Doesn't fly off the handle,
Doesn't keep score of the sins of others,
Doesn't revel when others grovel,
Takes pleasure in the flowering of truth,
Puts up with anything,
Trusts God always,
Always looks for the best,
Never looks back,

But keeps going to the end.

Love never dies. Inspired speech will be over some day; praying in tongues will end; understanding will reach its limit. We know only a portion of the truth, and what we say about God is always incomplete. But when the Complete arrives, our incompleteness will be canceled.

When I was an infant at my mother's breast, I gurgled and cooed like any infant. When I grew up, I left those infant ways for good.

We don't yet see things clearly. We're squinting in a fog, peering through a mist. But it won't be long before the weather clears and the sun shines bright! We'll see it all then, see it all as clearly as God sees us, knowing Him directly just as He knows us!

But for right now, until that completeness, we have three things to do to lead us toward that consummation: Trust steadily in God, hope unswervingly, love extravagantly. And the best of the three is love. (*The Message*)

What specifically can you DO to show others you care about them? What are we challenged to do in 1 John 3:18? What's the most important thing in this verse?

Father, I'm having a real hard time loving _____. But You created him (her), and I know as Your disciple, I need to be reflecting Your love.

Give me the strength to love, Lord. Help me put Your love into action. Are there some creative things I can be doing to reach out? Some simple, ordinary stuff I've overlooked? If so, please bring that to my mind.

I want people to KNOW I'm a Christian . . . by my love for those around me. Amen.

8

HOW CAN IT BE WRONG WHEN IT SEEMS SO RIGHT?

Glenn was in my third period English class. He was a big guy. Didn't really like school—or anyone in the human race for that matter. He was tough. His nickname was Mallard. (He waddled when he walked.) But he was proud of it. Even wrote it on all of his homework assignments . . . well, the two that he actually turned in that year!

Many of the students in my third and fifth period English classes weren't doing well with their grades. Now I knew most of these high school juniors cared more about "Green Day" than Henry David Thoreau, and more about last night's football scores than analyzing Emily Dickinson's poetry. But the reality was this: In five weeks, report cards would be issued, and if my students didn't get serious about their grades, many of them would fail.

So I created a fun plan to help them out. I created an extra study session that I called "The Breakfast Club" and announced that we would meet every Friday morning (I always gave English tests on Fridays) for the next five weeks. I explained that during this time, we'd go over the same information we'd studied all week, but because they would make an effort to come and study with me an extra thirty minutes before school, they'd receive an extra ten points on the test that day.

Not only that, but I'd provide all the donuts and juice they could down. Sounded like a good deal, and students were showing their excitement. There was one catch, though. "The Breakfast Club" would begin promptly at 7:30, but the door to my classroom would lock at 7:29. So to be involved, they had to arrive *before* 7:29. I knew Mallard was interested because he kept asking the same question every day: "Uh, what time is that breakfast club thing?" And I'd always respond, "Seven-thirty, Mallard. But you gotta be here before 7:29."

SOMEONE'S LATE!

Our first Friday finally arrived, and students began arriving at 7:15. I had purchased about one hundred donuts and began writing dates and information on the board. By 7:28 the class was filled, and at 7:29 I locked my door.

I began lecturing the same information I had taught all week. Kids were stuffing their faces with donuts and grinning from ear to ear. It was as if they finally realized there was HOPE. After all, I had told them if they came to "The Breakfast Club" during the next five weeks—and actually handed in their homework assignments, they'd probably pass. *They* were happy. *I* was happy.

Then suddenly, we heard someone jiggle the doorknob, loudly. Knocking followed. Then pounding. Then the whole door started rattling on its hinges. No problem. We just increased our noise level inside the classroom to drown out the sounds outside the classroom. Whatever was going on in the hallway wasn't nearly as important as what WE were doing. After all, we were eating free donuts, downing juice, and getting ten extra points for the test that day.

I dismissed the students about five minutes before first period, and as I walked past the office, the principal caught my attention. "Susie, did you hear all that noise outside your classroom this morning?"

"Yeah," I responded. "We didn't know what it was, and didn't want to take the time to find out, so we just kept plugging away."

"It was Mallard," he said. "Glenn had come to 'The Breakfast Club' but obviously arrived too late. When he realized he couldn't get in, he got angry and started screaming four-letter words, tried to knock the door down—and when *that* didn't work, brought in a crowbar and was trying to take the door off its hinges."

"Oh, brother!" I said.

"I suspended him," Mr. Griffis said. Then he laughed slightly. "And you know? That's the first time in the history of our school that a student has been suspended for coming to school early to study!"

I laughed too. Until I got back to my classroom. By then I wasn't laughing anymore. I was angry. I mean, I had created "The Breakfast Club" for kids *just like Mallard* who needed a second chance with their grades. I didn't have to do that. None of the *other* teachers were.

And I had provided the donuts and juice. And I had arrived an entire hour before school started, just to get everything ready. All Mallard had to do was simply obey the rules: Show up on time. And he didn't even do *that!* Now he was suspended and who knew if he would *ever* pass? All because he was disobedient.

A few hours later, though, God began working in my thoughts. It's as if He wanted to give me a reminder of the strong penalty disobedience brings. There's *always* a price to pay for being disobedient. It's written all through the Bible.

But Mallard's Not the Only One

There's an interesting story in the book of 1 Samuel. Look at what chapter 15 is all about. Quick synopsis: God had just given Saul and his men the strength to defeat an extremely wicked nation. Because of their evil ways, God wanted this nation and *everything* in it *to be destroyed.* He didn't want any trace of wickedness left. Everything meant everything. Even the sheep and cattle.

Well, Saul disobeyed God. He did *not* destroy all the sheep and cattle. He said, "Nah. Let's keep the best cattle. And surely God wouldn't want us to waste the fattest sheep."

Hmmm. Makes sense. I mean, would God really want Saul to destroy even the best animals? The more Saul rationalized, the more it made sense to disobey God's command.

Somehow we believe if we can make it make sense, it's okay. We *love* to make sense, don't we? It's a dangerous temptation to try to make sense out of disobeying God!

Maybe you've even heard yourself saying, "This makes sense, so let's do it!"

Who cares if it makes sense or not? The issue isn't whether it makes sense. The issue is: *Are you obeying God?* You see, God doesn't always make sense . . . at least not *human* sense—only godly sense. Here are a few examples of things God says that don't make sense to our earthly minds:

- The first shall be last.
- The last shall be first.
- Lose your life to find it.
- The greatest shall be the least.
- Give away to receive.

None of these make sense at first glance. As we get to know God better, though, we begin to understand His ways.

IT'S NOT ALWAYS SMART TO MAKE SENSE

Saul and his men disobeyed God. They made a lot of sense, but they were still disobedient. In fact, because Saul thought his actions were so logical, he didn't even bother to HIDE all the animals they'd kept.

When the godly prophet Samuel found Saul, this is how Saul greeted him: *The Lord bless you! I've carried out his commands!*

Just like us, huh? We do something wrong and try to cover up by acting really positive, don't we?

The story is found in 1 Samuel 13–16. I imagine the conversation went something like this:

"You've carried out His commands? Then what's all this sheep bleating I'm hearing? And, Saul, I gotta tell you, man, I'm hearing a few hundred moos, too."

Saul cleared his throat—maybe even took a sip of Gatorade from his canteen, then defended himself. "Well . . . we spared the best of the sheep and cattle to sacrifice to the Lord. But we totally destroyed the rest!"

At that point, Samuel told Saul to put a lid on it (the Gatorade *and* his mouth) and give him a quick review of what God's instructions had been. Then he concluded by giving Saul the bottom line.

Bottom line: "You didn't obey God, Saul!"

Well, Saul didn't like that. (Just like *we* don't like being told *we've* done it wrong, either! So he tried to make himself sound good.)

"Yes, I did! I defeated this town and destroyed all these idols and I did . . ."

Halfway's Not Good Enough

Well, he had partially obeyed God. But that's not enough, is it? It's like brushing your teeth. From your very first trip to the dentist when you hear him say, "Brush your teeth at *least* twice a day," you know he means ALL your teeth. Can you imagine what he'd say during your next visit upon finding two cavities?

"Wow, looks like you've got a couple of holes we're gonna have to fill. Have you been brushing regularly?"

"Yeah."

"You have? Really?"

You clear your throat and shift a little in that weird chair. "Well, yeah. Maybe not twice a day. And, OK, I don't always brush *all* of them."

"What do you mean you don't always brush all of them?"

"Well, I'm busy. I have band practice and stuff to do with my friends. So sometimes I rotate which teeth I brush. Last week, for instance, I brushed the top row of teeth on Monday and Wednesday, and the bottom row on Tuesday and Thursday."

"What about Friday, Saturday and Sunday?" he asks.

"Hey! That's my weekend. Don't crowd me."

He'd probably tell you to find yourself another dentist. Only brushing *part* of your teeth just isn't good enough, is it? Works the same way in your relationship with Christ. It's not enough to obey God a little. He wants to be LORD, and that requires one hundred percent obedience.

Again, what Saul and his men had done made sense. It made a lot of sense to offer as a sacrifice (offering) to God the best cattle and the fattest sheep. *But it was all done in disobedience!*

And then Samuel hit Saul with a real zinger: "Has the Lord as much pleasure in your burnt offerings and sacrifices as in your obedience? Obedience is far better than sacrifice. He is much more interested in your listening to him than in your offering the fat of rams to him" (1 Samuel 15:22, TLB).

Saul stammered around, shifting his weight along with his beady little eyes while Samuel continued. "For rebellion is as bad as the sin of witchcraft, and stubbornness is as bad as worshiping idols" (1 Samuel 15:23, TLB).

IS IT REALLY THAT BAD?

WOW! Disobeying God is as bad as witchcraft?

"And now because you have rejected the word of Jehovah, he has rejected you from being king" (1 Samuel 15:23, TLB).

THAT got Saul's attention! When we realize what we're not going to get, we learn real fast, don't we? So he finally decided to come clean.

"I have sinned. . . . Yes, I have disobeyed your instructions and the command of the Lord, for I was afraid of the people and did what they demanded" (1 Samuel 15:24, TLB).

Well, it's one thing to come clean—it's another thing to blame our disobedience on those around us. But at least Saul was headed in the right direction. Samuel probably inserted a few powerful words on peer pressure. (If *you* need a little encouragement on taking a stand, cruise over to chapter one.)

Again, Saul's sin was not illogical. It wasn't that he couldn't make sense out of what he did. His sin was that *he disobeyed* God.

We *cannot* rationalize God's instructions, commands, or will. Sometimes His ways don't make sense . . . and again, it's not our responsibility to understand God's ways. *Our* job is to simply obey His leading.

Adam and Eve disobeyed God in the Garden of Eden. He specifically told them *not* to eat from a certain tree. They did, though, and felt tremendous guilt. We've been disobeying and feeling guilty ever since. And it's when we wrestle with guilt that we do a million different things to try to erase it. We blame it on those around us (like Saul), or we say we didn't really understand in the first place. Some of us try to forget our sins by adding MORE sin on top of the wrong we're involved in. Some hide— like Adam, who tried to cover himself with a leaf.

TRYING TO ERASE GUILT

Still others go to even further extremes. I once read an Oklahoma City magazine article about people who actually send money to the government because of a guilty conscience. It all started back in 1811 when the first guilty soul sent $5 and an apology during the presidency of James Madison. Since that time, over 79 million dollars has been sent in voluntarily to the U.S. government.

Since so much money has been voluntarily sent to the government in the past few years, the Treasury Department finally created a special fund for donations. "The Conscience Fund" includes money from people who say they once cheated the government and are trying to erase their guilt. Payments are usually accompanied by confessions and are usually anonymous. Some have cheated on their income taxes; others have recycled an uncanceled postage stamp. There are also those who have slipped souvenirs or other items past U.S. Customs Service officers without paying duty on them.

One former GI sent in $150 (this was about six years ago) for unauthorized items he had brought home from overseas after his discharge from the army way back in 1946! (Guilt has a way of staying with us, doesn't it?)

Someone else sent in $100 for damaging some fire fighting equipment at an army site in Maryland several years ago. One citizen donated $1,075 for not declaring jewelry to a Customs officer.

All of these people are trying to dissolve the guilt caused from disobedience. When we disobey God, it's a big deal! Throughout the Word, we see that He consistently punishes the disobedient. Saul's kingdom was destroyed because of it. Achan died because of it. Adam and Eve were cast out of the garden because of it. *You will not be the exception!*

STUFF YOU DON'T HAVE TO PRAY ABOUT

You don't have to pray about whether God meant what He said—even when it doesn't make sense. Many Christians spend a lot of time praying over things God has already made explicitly clear in His Word. (Saul probably wrestled back and forth about whether he should destroy EVERYTHING. God had already given very clear instructions. There was no need for Saul to pray about it or wrestle over it.)

Are there things in *your* life that God is already dealing with you about? If so, don't spend your time praying about whether to obey. Don't sit around trying to make it all make sense. Instead, ask Christ to strengthen you through the power of His Holy Spirit to consistently obey Him, whether or not it makes sense.

Stuff You Should Pray About

Since you're human, you're not perfect. It's just a plain, simple fact that you're going to blow it from time to time. Simply meet God in prayer, confess your disobedience, and continue walking with Him.

Instead, pray for:

1. Forgiveness. The same God who punishes the sin of disobedience, is the same Father who forgives all who repent.

Ammunition: For proof-positive that God wants to forgive our disobedience, sneak a peek at Hebrews 10:22. After you've read it, read it again.

Notice the 1-2-3 approach in this passage. (Makes it really easy to understand, doesn't it?)

1. Come to God with a sincere heart.

2. Repent.

3. His promise: To cleanse us from guilt!

Did you catch that last part of the promise? We don't have to spend time praying and praying and begging and begging God to take away the guilt. He's already got it under control—has already made plans to rid you of guilt and replace it with joy and forgiveness.

It's like you telling your best friend that you want to treat her to a Coca-Cola after school. When she talks with you between classes or sends you notes, she doesn't need to spend that time asking and begging you to take her for a Coke after school. You've already promised you would. All she has to do is come. Instead, she could be spending her time in conversation with you about things you really need to talk about. (See how that relates to prayer and all the stuff God has already covered?)

2. Assurance that you are forgiven. It doesn't matter how many times you've disobeyed God, or what's hiding in your past . . . God *will* forgive! And what's more, He even lets you share in His inheritance of eternal life.

Ammunition: Titus 3:3. Copy it on a note card and read it over and over and over again for assurance of your forgiveness and your eternal inheritance. Notice how generous God is in this passage.

1. He forgives.

2. He forgets.

3. He brings us out of past guilt and blesses us with freedom.

4. He justifies us (*justification* means *just-as-if-I'd* never sinned).

5. He gives us the inheritance of eternal life.

3. Pray for the DESIRE to obey. God has the power to help us *want* to obey Him. Even when we don't feel like it we must obey, but He can give us the desire. Why not *ask* Him for that desire?

Ammunition: Philippians 2:13 (memorize it!): "For God is at work within you, helping you want to obey him, and then helping you do what he wants" (TLB).

Lord, I realize now that ALL disobedience is a big deal. Whether I'm copying answers off of someone's English test or whether I steal a car, I'm disobeying You. I guess maybe it's the small things I ought to begin with. Help me to be faithful and obedient to Your leading in the ordinary, daily stuff so I can learn to be more consistently obedient in the bigger things of life.

I never thought I'd say this, but thanks for guilt. I want to feel bad when I do something wrong. But thanks that I don't have to live with guilt—that You'll forgive and release me from my sin as soon as I confess.

Thanks so much for Your generosity, Father. And for the freedom I can have when I live obediently in Your will every day. I love you, Jesus. Help me to be all You want me to be. Amen.

STUFF TO GROW ON #4

Ready for some spiritual "vitamins" from the New Testament? Copy the following verses on index cards (or if you're feeling creative, get some paper with adhesive backing and make your own bumper stickers) and place them in key places where you'll see them often (the cover of your notebook, your backpack, wallet or purse, inside your locker, etc.), and let them serve as positive reminders to keep your mind focused in the right direction.

I am with you; that is all you need. My power shows up best in weak people (2 Corinthians 12:9, TLB).

For whatever God says to us is full of living power: it is sharper than the sharpest dagger, cutting swift and deep into our innermost thoughts and desires with all their parts, exposing us for what we really are.

He knows about everyone, everywhere. Everything about us is bare and wide open to the all-seeing eyes of our living God; nothing can be hidden from him to whom we must explain all that we have done (Hebrews 4:12–13, TLB).

Don't let anyone think little of you because you are young. Be their ideal; let them follow the way you teach and live; be a pattern for them in your love, your faith, and your clean thoughts (1 Timothy 4:12, TLB).

For God did not call us to be impure, but to live a holy life (1 Thessalonians 4:7, NIV).

For God is not a God of disorder but of peace (1 Corinthians 14:33, NIV).

Now glory be to God who by his mighty power at work within us is able to do far more than we would ever dare to ask or even dream of—infinitely beyond our highest prayers, desires, thoughts, or hopes (Ephesians 3:20, TLB).

9

DISCOVERING GOD'S WILL

My grandma was an excellent nurse. She lovingly cared for hundreds of patients over the course of several years, and hearing her recount the stories of how she helped sick people feel better made such an impression on my six-year-old mind, that I decided that's what *I* wanted to be—until I decided the guy who drove the neighborhood ice cream truck had a much more exciting profession.

Then, when I was in the fifth grade, I wanted to be an explorer. (We had just finished studying Lewis and Clark and I was ready to carve some trails.)

By the seventh grade I knew I was going to be an oceanographer, but by my junior year in high school, I had switched to becoming a tennis pro. But to be honest, I still wasn't satisfied. I had spent a lot of time in prayer seeking God's will for my life and had told the Lord I wanted His best plan—not my own.

By my senior year in high school, when I still didn't know what God's will was, I gave the Lord an ultimatum. After all, we're told in James 1:5 to expect an answer when we ask God what to do. So, I expected. I told God I wanted to know His exact will for my life in one week. (I figured if He could whip up a couple of humans out of dust, set the world in motion, and hang the stars in place all in a good seven days, giving me a hint about my future would be no big deal.)

OH, IS THAT WHAT YOU WANT?

As I waited for His answer, I also spent more time in prayer and reading the Bible. Toward the end of the week, a funny thing happened. God began to talk to me but not in a thundering voice.

Sometimes He used my thoughts as I read His Word. Verses took on new meaning; things seemed clearer in my mind. I began to realize this was God's voice, His special way of helping me understand and communicate with Him.

I read Habakkuk 2:3. "But these things I plan won't happen right away. Slowly, steadily, surely, the time approaches when the vision will be fulfilled. If it seems slow, do not despair, for these things will surely come to pass. Just be patient! They will not be overdue a single day!" (TLB)

Whoa! So, naturally I began to think, *Who am I to put a time limit on the Creator of the universe?* He also showed me through Hebrews 6:12 that by being so concerned about His will for my future, I was missing out on His will for *today!*

My prayer changed. Instead of worrying about what I would do for a career, I began to pray, "Lord, help me to be all You want me to be *right now.*"

Guess what? As I concentrated on being in the center of His will *one day at a time*, He began to reveal (in bits and pieces) His dreams for my future.

Maybe you, too, are interested in a variety of things and are struggling with narrowing down your future goals. Your friends know what they want to do and how they're going to achieve it. That's okay. Don't get stressed out just because you don't. Instead, ask God to help you become all He wants you to be right now.

GOD'S WILL ISN'T A JOB

See, my big mistake was thinking "God's will" meant my career. Actually, our vocation is only a small part of God's will for our lives. God's will also includes:

- your impact on those around you
- the people you date
- how you treat your family
- if you'll marry or remain single
- who you'll marry
- where you'll live
- the type of person you'll become
- how you'll raise your children
- _____ (You fill in a few. There are a whole lot more!)

Know what the Apostle Paul's vocation was? He was a tent-maker. Think he spent time praying about whether God wanted him to live a holy life? Nope. Living like Christ has *nothing* to do with our career. Reflecting Jesus is our number one, absolute, most important, MAJOR reason to live. Our career—no matter what it is—is merely something we do on the side. Our main FOCUS is to be Jesus to the world around us. That's God's will for our lives.

MISSING THE CLUES

Perhaps at this point you're saying, "But what if I MISS what God has in store for my future because I take a wrong turn or something?"

Remember this: Christ paid a mighty BIG price for you. Think He's going to let you miss out on His best that easily? No way.

Imagine your dad lost his job. Your mom's part-time position at the local bank isn't enough to support your entire family. You receive a phone call informing you that you've just won a million dollars for some off-the-wall contest you entered about six months ago. The money is being given away by an eccentric billionaire. He explains that he's going to deliver the money—in cash. There are a couple of weird things about this contest, though. First, you can't actually *keep* the money, but must give it to your family. Second, you can't just GIVE it to them, you have to hide it and give them clues as to where it can be found.

No problem. You would've given the money to your dad anyway. Your family *needs* it right now, and you're excited to help out. So you carefully wrap the money in a metal box and hide it near the sandbox in the backyard.

You write a poem filled with clues about where the treasure can be found. They venture into the backyard. If you see them heading toward the old oak tree in the corner, you'll probably steer them away from that and toward the sandbox. And if they mean-der into the garage, you'll coax them out and in the direction of the sandbox. When they saunter over to the swing set, you'll gen-tly guide them back to the sand. And as they rush to the garden, you'll probably take their hands and pull them toward the money.

You'll do everything you can to make sure they know exactly where the treasure is. It works the same way with God's will. When He wants you to do something, He'll give you a million and one clues to head you in the right direction. And when you start to veer off to the side, He may shut the door in your face. Don't panic. Simply realize it's His way of turning you around. Change direction and notice that He's opened a window for you to climb through.

He'll even take your hand and *guide* you . . . if you'll ask Him. He has way too much invested in His plan for your life to let you just "not get it."

He's even given you a map: "The whole Bible was given to us by inspiration from God and is useful to teach us what is true and to make us realize what is wrong in our lives; it straightens us out and helps us do what is right. It is God's way of making us well prepared at every point, fully equipped to do good to every-one" (2 Timothy 3:16–17, TLB).

STUFF YOU DON'T HAVE TO PRAY ABOUT

Settled. You don't have to:

- Plead with God about where your life is going to be ten years from now. *Christ wants you to focus on being all He wants right now!*
- Worry about whom you'll marry. *God is big enough to bring just the right person along at just the right time.*
- Beg God to lead you in a specific direction. *Trust HIM to fulfill your heart's desires.*

STUFF YOU SHOULD PRAY ABOUT

Why use your creative energy worrying about the future when instead you can throw yourself into making the most out of your *present*? Spend time praying about:

1. Using the gifts and abilities God has blessed you with. Feel like He's leading you into some kind of music ministry? Then instead of becoming obsessed with being Amy Grant's new duet partner, focus on being the best soprano (or bass) your church choir has ever had.

Do you think that maybe God is leading you into accounting? Instead of demanding to take over the family budget, run for class treasurer, or volunteer to organize the books for your youth group's fund-raising projects.

You're sensing Christ is calling you into preaching? Instead of becoming a loud-mouthed, in-your-face know-it-all to the kids around you at school, simply speak the truth in love. And make yourself available for praying before football games, track meets, and sharing your testimony at before-school Bible clubs.

In other words, allow God to make you the *best you can be* **right where you are!** It's not being in the spotlight or making money carrying out God's will that makes the Father smile. It's being all you can be in the center of His will RIGHT NOW that makes Him proud.

Ammunition: Check out Ephesians 4:11–14. Recognize any of your gifts in here? What about the list in Romans 12:6–8?

2. Believing in HIS dreams for your life. You serve a God who wants your fulfillment even more than you do! Therefore, He dreams bigger dreams for you than you would ever dare create for yourself. You serve a GIANT of a God; therefore, learn to think BIG.

Ammunition: Read Ephesians 3:20. Is this proof-positive that your Father dreams B-I-G dreams for you, or what? Need more proof? Try memorizing Jeremiah 29:11 in a COUPLE of different versions:

> "For I know the plans I have for you, says the Lord. They are plans for good and not for evil, to give you a future and a hope"(TLB).

> " 'For I know the plans I have for you,' declares the Lord, plans to prosper you and not to harm you, plans to give you 'hope and a future' " (NIV).

> "I alone know the plans I have for you, plans to bring you prosperity and not disaster, plans to bring about the future you hope for" (TEV).

But what if you think God is calling you to the mission field? Again, the most important thing in your life is to be 100 percent sold-out to Him right now. If He's really LORD, it doesn't matter WHERE He wants to send you next year or ten years from now.

It could be He WILL send you to the mission field. Or it might be that He simply wants to know that your answer is "Yes, Lord" to *anything* He asks of you. Sometimes God leads us in a specific direction, then changes our course at a later date. The issue isn't where you're going, it's *who* you're going with!

Father, I admit many times I'm super-anxious about my future. I worry and question and doubt. Forgive me for that. I WANT to relax and simply trust You.

I realize that my career is only a small part of "Your will" for my life. So help me to concentrate on being committed to You every single day beginning right now. Amen.

10

BUT I'M NOT RICH!

He had a funny name: Haggai. (Pronounced: Hey, Guy!) And he had a unique career: prophet. (His job was to tell people about God and warn them about what would happen if they didn't follow His leading.) Surprisingly, people listened to his message. Maybe they listened because everything was messed up. We have a tendency to do that, don't we? When things get reallyreallyreally bad, we're finally ready to listen to someone tell us how to get back on track again.

The time? 538 B.C.

The place? Jerusalem.

The situation? God's temple was in ruins.

The background? Babylonian armies had destroyed the temple—God's house. Several years later, the Jews were granted permission to return to their homeland to rebuild the temple. They excitedly made the journey and began the construction process. But it was hot outside. And they wanted to work on building their own homes, too. Some of them decided to plant gardens and join the J.C.C. (Jerusalem Country Club)—they offered a terrific price to families joining during the summer months. Others enlisted in summer softball leagues and went camping.

NOT A PRETTY SIGHT

The result? Their priorities shifted. What once was their purpose now became only a past hobby. Apparently no one minded going to church in a temple that was falling apart. Didn't bother them that the air conditioner squeaked, the back wall was missing, and that only twenty-three of the five hundred pews were left standing (and *those* had tons of splinters). No one cared that the heater pumped out rust instead of heat, mice had taken over the carpet, the communion table only had one leg, and that no one was doing anything for missions.

There were advantages to the sun roof, though. Basically, there was no roof—which meant the youth group often bragged about getting a tan during the service. In short, this church was pitiful. And what's really sad is that it was GOD'S HOUSE—a symbol of His presence with them. He was the one who had freed them from captivity and allowed them to go back to their homeland. Wouldn't you think they'd be grateful?

He was the one who had kept them safe during the journey, provided good leaders for them, and met their every need. Wouldn't you think after all God had given them, that they'd want to give back to God?

Well, you'd think so. But again . . . we have to remember their priorities were out of whack. Even though God had given them the specific assignment of building His temple, they had put it on the back burner. They'd lost His vision . . . didn't take Him seriously.

OUR MAN FOR THE HOUR

That's when Haggai entered the scene. And even though it was forever ago (well, almost forever . . . twenty-five centuries), his message still rings clear today.

He didn't cut any corners and told the people exactly what they needed to hear. (Which wasn't necessarily what they wanted to hear.) He knew most of the population gathered around the city square for pizza on Friday nights, so he borrowed one of those megaphones from a JHS cheerleader (Jerusalem High School), and around 7:00 P.M., he let them have it.

"Why is everyone saying it's not the right time to rebuild the temple?" he said.

One guy choked on his pepperoni-with-extra-pepperoni pizza. Someone else raised his hand and asked for more Parmesan. Another man shouted, "Hey! Guy! While you're up front, mind gettin' me a refill on this Coke?"

Haggai ignored him and repeated the question with more force. "Why are you all saying this isn't the right time to rebuild the temple?"

"The temple?" asked a waitress.

"It's Friday night," moaned Dave. "This is the only time I have to relax and eat pizza and forget about finals."

"Yeah," said Jamie. "It's my night off. I don't wanna think about rebuilding the temple."

"Too much work," said another.

"I'd get dirty."

Well, Haggai had had it! But he didn't let up. (After all, this was his job. He was a prophet, remember? And he took his responsibility seriously.)

He reminded them of how bad things were. It was easy to forget their problems while munching on pizza and downing breadsticks, but Haggai brought them back to reality.

"Too bad you never have enough money," he said. And Geoff groaned. Seemed like he'd been saving forever to get a new mountain bike. Still didn't have enough.

"And too bad your clothes are old and worn out," Haggai continued. Allison rolled her eyes. How well she knew *that*.

"And too bad you work so hard," Haggai said, "to get back so little."

Coach Mueller sighed. He had a family to support and a new baby on the way. He worked hard. In fact, he even worked overtime. Never could make ends meet, though.

"Probably feel like you're living in a rut, don't you?" Haggai said. "An endless cycle. You get up. You go to school or work. You put in a full day. You come home. No purpose. No real happiness. Don't have what you *need*, and can't have what you *want*."

By now most people had wiped the tomato paste off their chins. A few were still chewing on ice from the bottom of their Coke glasses, but they were listening.

So Haggai let 'em have it. "God has commanded that you build the temple, yet you sit around week after week and say, 'It's just not the right time.' Well, when will it be the right time?"

Even though they were all late for the T.G.I.F. lineup on Friday night TV, no one checked his watch.

"If you'll simply give God what is His (obedience, and at least 10 percent of your time to rebuilding the temple), He'll give back to you more than you can imagine!"

STILL LISTENING

Hmmm. We can't outgive God. It was a concept worth chewing on.

Haggai continued, "So what *is* it the right time for? Is it the right time for stuffing yourselves with pizza when God's temple lies in ruin? Is it the right time for building on to your home, planting gardens, planning expensive vacations, or buying a car when the temple needs repairing? GET YOUR PRIORITIES STRAIGHT!"

Mr. Andrews raised his hand. "OK, we hear you, Haggai. We'll start praying for God to give us the desire to rebuild His temple."

"Why do you have to pray about it?" Haggai asked. "God has already commanded that you do it."

"Yeah, but we gotta want to," piped Mrs. Ward.

"I don't think so," Haggai continued. "Whether you *want to* has absolutely nothing to do with God's command. Just do it!" (An advertising executive from NIKE athletic shoes just happened to be in the crowd that day and later decided to use this as a popular ad slogan.)

Well, it was late. People were restless. Many of them left, deciding to pray for the desire to rebuild the temple. "When God gives us the *desire* to do it, we'll obey," someone said.

But some of the people—the ones who were really listening—heard God's voice through Haggai. And they obeyed. Even though they didn't have a burning desire to rebuild the temple, they did it anyway because God had commanded them to.

And guess what? *After* they started putting the temple together, *God blessed them with the desire!*

STUFF YOU DON'T HAVE TO PRAY ABOUT

Seems like we have it all backwards, doesn't it? How often do we catch ourselves thinking, *I'll pray for the desire to invite Ashley to church, or the desire to get more involved in my youth group, or the desire to read my Bible more. And when God gives me the desire, I'll do it.*

But that's backwards. Desire isn't part of the command. The issue is WILL YOU OBEY GOD EVEN WHEN YOU DON'T FEEL LIKE IT? If so, just do it! And God will bless you with the desire to CONTINUE doing it after you've started.

What are we talking about here? Repainting the walls in your youth room at church? Could be. But there's a much deeper issue I want you to focus on. And that's the issue of *tithing*. It's clear that God has commanded you to build His temple. How do you do that? One way is by supporting His work through your tithes and offerings. This is how His temple—the church, God's kingdom—is built and enabled to grow.

Well, just how much money are we talking about when we talk tithe?

Good question. If you claim to be a Christian, then God really owns everything you have, doesn't He? (This is where you're supposed to answer yes or nod your head in the affirmative.) But He only asks that you give a minimum of 10 percent back to Him. Ten percent out of 100. Not bad . . . considering *all* we own really belongs to Him.

"The purpose of tithing is to teach you always to put God first in your lives" (Deuteronomy 14:23, TLB).

"The people responded immediately and generously . . . a tithe of all they owned, as required by law to be given to the Lord their God" (2 Chronicles 31:5–6, TLB).

STUFF YOU SHOULD PRAY ABOUT

You don't have to spend time praying about whether God wants you to tithe. He's already made it clear: *build my temple!* And one of the most important ways you do that is by giving tithes and offerings. So spend time instead praying about:

1. Giving more than money. Instead of simply giving 10 percent of all you earn, why not consider giving away a few other things as well.

YOUR TIME: Volunteer to babysit free for a couple in your neighborhood who would love to have an evening out. Or offer to walk the neighbor's dog.

Ammunition: Philippians 2:3–7. What kind of attitude should you have?

YOUR SKILLS: Could you offer to redecorate a few of the bulletin boards at church? Clean an elderly person's house?

YOUR GENEROSITY: Walk a few dogs in your neighborhood, bake cookies for a shut-in, send your pastor a fun note with a two-dollar bill inside (yes, they are available at the bank), and don't tell him who it's from.

Ammunition: Colossians 3:23–24. What kind of attitude should you have when thinking of others? What kind of reward will you receive?

YOUR CREATIVITY: Get a child's lunch box at the mall and pack it full of surprises (microwave popcorn, a fun pen and pencil, sticky notes, licorice sticks, bubble gum) and mail it to someone who's lonely; create a collage expressing your appreciation for your Sunday School teacher, youth minister, or parents; get a box of doggie treats for a dog in your neighborhood, wrap them in newspaper, and present them to the owner.

Ammunition: Philippians 2:1. What does God say about cheering each other up?

2. Gain a proper perspective of your money. Who's really in charge of your finances? Don't cling to something that's only temporary.

Ammunition: Mark 10:21–23. What does this passage say about the importance of money?

3. Giving to someone less fortunate. Compassion International has a wonderful child sponsorship program. For only $24 a month, you (or you and your youth group) can give a child an education, school supplies, a school uniform, and a hot meal once a day. Your child will write you letters, send you his report card, and let you know how you can pray specifically for him. Call 1-800-336-7676 for an information packet.

Ammunition: Matthew 25:34–46. How will God reward your willingness to help others? When you reach out to someone else, who are you really touching?

Father, sometimes I become selfish with what I have. Please help me to remember that ALL I have is really

Yours. I want to do my part in building Your Kingdom, and I realize that it all starts with my willingness to give back to You *at least* 10 percent of all I earn. I commit that from this day forward, I will be consistent in giving tithes and offerings. Amen.

STUFF TO GROW ON #5

For more exciting thoughts on giving, check out the following story by a woman named Edie Ogan.

THE RICH FAMILY IN OUR CHURCH

I'll never forget Easter 1946. I was fourteen, my little sister Ocy, twelve, and my older sister, Darlene, was sixteen. We lived at home with our mother, and the four of us knew what it was to do without many things.

My dad had died five years before, leaving Mom with seven school kids to raise and no money. By 1946 my older sisters were married, and my brothers had left home.

A month before Easter, the pastor of our church announced that a special Easter offering would be taken to help a poor family. He asked everyone to save and give sacrificially.

When we got home, we talked about what we could do. We decided to buy fifty pounds of potatoes and live on them for a month. This would allow us to save twenty dollars of our grocery money for the offering.

Then we thought that if we kept our electric lights turned out as much as possible and didn't listen to the radio, we'd save money on that month's electric bill. Darlene got as many house-cleaning and yard jobs as possible, and both of us babysat for everyone we could. For fifteen cents, we could buy enough cotton loops to make three pot holders to sell for one dollar. We made twenty dollars on pot holders.

That month was one of the best of our lives. Every day we counted the money to see how much we had saved. At night we'd sit in the dark and talk about how the poor family was going to enjoy having the money the church would give them. We had about eighty people in church, so we figured that whatever amount of money we had to give, the offering would surely be twenty times that much. After all, every Sunday the pastor had reminded everyone to save for the sacrificial offering.

The day before Easter, Ocy and I walked to the grocery store and got the manager to give us three crisp twenty dollar bills and one ten dollar bill for all our change. We ran all the way home to show Mom and Darlene. We had never had so much money before.

That night we were so excited we could hardly sleep. We didn't care that we wouldn't have new clothes for Easter; we had seventy dollars for the sacrificial offering. We could hardly wait to get to church!

On Sunday morning, rain was pouring. We didn't own an umbrella, and the church was over a mile from our home, but it didn't seem to matter how wet we got. Darlene had cardboard in her shoes to fill the holes. The cardboard came apart, and her feet got wet, but we sat in church proudly. I heard some teenagers talking about us having on old dresses. I looked at them in their new clothes, and I felt so rich.

When the sacrificial offering was taken, we were sitting on the second row from the front. Mom put in the ten dollar bill, and each of us girls put in a twenty-dollar bill. As we walked home after church, we sang all the way. At lunch Mom had a surprise for us. She had bought a dozen eggs, and we had boiled Easter eggs with our fried potatoes!

Late that afternoon the minister drove up in his car. Mom went to the door, talked with him for a moment, and then came back with an envelope in her hand. We asked what it was, but she didn't say a word. She opened the envelope and out fell a bunch of money. There were three crisp twenty-dollar bills, one ten-dollar bill, and seventeen one dollar bills.

Mom put the money back in the envelope. We didn't talk, just sat and stared at the floor. We had gone from feeling like millionaires to feeling like poor white trash.

We kids had had such a happy life that we felt sorry for anyone who didn't have our mom and dad for parents and a house full of brothers and sisters and other kids visiting constantly. We thought it was fun to share silverware and see whether we got the fork or the spoon that night. We had two knives which we passed around to whoever needed them.

I knew we didn't have a lot of things that other people had, but I'd never thought that we were poor. That Easter Day I found we were. The minister had brought us the money for the poor family, so we must be poor.

I didn't like being poor. I looked at my dress and worn-out shoes and felt so ashamed that I didn't want to go back to church. Everyone there probably already knew we were poor! I thought about school. I was in the ninth grade and at the top of my class of over one hundred students. I wondered if the kids at school knew we were poor. I decided I could quit school since I had finished the eighth grade. That was all the law required at that time.

We sat in silence for a long time. Then it got dark, and we went to bed. All that week, we girls went to school and came home, and no one talked much. Finally on Saturday, Mom asked us what we wanted to do with the money. What did poor people do with money? We didn't know. We'd never known we were poor.

We didn't want to go to church on Sunday, but Mom said

we had to. Although it was a sunny day, we didn't talk on the way. Mom started to sing, but no one joined in, and she only sang one verse.

At church we had a missionary speaker. He talked about how churches in Africa made buildings out of sun-dried bricks, but they needed money to buy roofs. He said $100 would put a roof on a church. The minister said, "Can't we all sacrifice to help these poor people?"

We looked at each other and smiled for the first time in a week. Mom reached into her purse and pulled out the envelope. She passed it to Darlene. Darlene gave it to me, and I handed it to Ocy. Ocy put it in the offering plate.

When the offering was counted, the minister announced that it was a little over $100. The missionary was excited. He hadn't expected such a large offering from our small church. He said, "You must have some rich people in this church."

Suddenly it struck us! We had given $87 of the "little over $100." We were the rich family in the church! Hadn't the missionary said so?

From that day on I've never been poor again. I've always remembered how rich I am because I have Jesus.[1]

Notes

1. *This story by Edie Ogan was first published in* Mountain Movers, *a foreign missions magazine published by the Assemblies of God Church.*

11

Trials and Tough Times

My friend Jan went to Alaska last year. I teasingly asked her to bring me back something, and when she returned I was given a pamphlet, *Bear Facts: The Essentials for Traveling in Bear Country.*

Since my parents had been trying to talk me into going to Alaska with them for vacation, I was anxious to see what *Bear Country* was all about. Though in all seriousness this leaflet was written to help tourists prepare for possible bear encounters, I couldn't help laughing as I read through it. (I think that's why she brought it back for me. She knew what a kick I'd get out of reading it.)

I found out that three species of American bears flourish in our fiftieth state. Now I'm not particularly anxious to see a bear—or even get *near* one for that matter—but according to my bear facts, "There is a chance you may be lucky enough to see a bear. But even if you don't, you will never be far from one, because Alaska is bear country."

Hmmm. Not real comforting.

I read on. "Bears are curious, intelligent and potentially dangerous animals, but in most cases, if you give a bear the opportunity to do the right thing, it will."

And I'm wondering about the other cases. You know, those times when Mr. Bear's just feeling a bit mischievous.

"A study showed that during the first eighty-five years of this century, only twenty people died in bear attacks in Alaska. During 1975-1985, however, ten people in Alaska were killed by dogs."

Great, I'm thinking. *If the bears don't get me, a dog will! I better warn my parents.*

I continued reading. "Bears don't like surprises!" Like what? Someone would actually TRY to catch a bear off guard? BOO! I don't think so.

"Don't crowd bears. Give them plenty of room! Every bear has a personal space." I don't think I know anyone who would argue, "Hey, beat it! I was here first" if they were approached by a five-foot, 400-pound black bear.

By now I couldn't put the pamphlet down. "Bears are always looking for something to eat." Oh, now *there's* a nice thought!

"If a bear approaches you while fishing, STOP FISHING." Like I wouldn't have thought of that myself?

"If you have a fish on your line, don't let it splash!" Shhh. There's a bear behind us. Keep it down, will you?

"If it's not possible to keep the fish from splashing, cut your line." I don't know about YOU, but if I'm fishing and a bear approaches, I'm not taking time to look around for a knife to cut my line. I'm throwing the whole thing in the lake and jumping in with it.

"If you see a bear, avoid it if you can." Now THAT'S handy-dandy advice.

"Identify yourself. Let the bear know you are human. Help the bear recognize you." Hi, I'm Susie. Wanna see my license?

And finally . . . "You can't outrun a bear." You look like an animal who likes to run. Wanna race?

I laughed through that entire pamphlet. And even though it was filled with stuff I thought was funny, it also contained some valuable information about what to really do if attacked by a bear.

The only place I've seen a bear is in the zoo . . . but many times I feel as if I'm having a "bear attack" because of a tough time or trial I'm experiencing.

LIFE IS WHAT YOU MAKE IT

No one enjoys tough times, and it seems some people go through more than their share. Here are a few examples of tough times and how people responded:

• About five years ago, my friend Jackie lost her mother unexpectedly. A year later, Jackie had a miscarriage. The following year, her sister died. Again, unexpectedly, Jackie had another miscarriage. I wanted to scream for her. My heart pleaded, *why?* Through it all, though, Jackie's relationship with Christ remained constant.

• When Bobby was a junior in high school, his little brother was killed in a car accident. Bobby's reaction? "If this is what Christianity's all about, I want nothing to do with it." He turned his back on God.

• Brent was enjoying life as a high school student when a tumor was detected in his left arm. He had to have it amputated. Just a couple of years later, in college, a doctor noticed a spot on his lung. Cancer. Through the questions and tears, however, Brent's faith in God never wavered.

• Kelli's dad left the family when she was eleven years old. Because she was the oldest, she felt a responsibility to help care for her younger brothers and sisters. Her mom had to work two jobs just to make ends meet. Night after night, Kelli prayed for her dad's return. He never came back. She quit going to Sunday

School and church. "God doesn't exist," she said, "or my family wouldn't have this many problems."

• I met fourteen-year-old Rose on a trip to Uganda. I saw her singing, dancing, and playing sports with the other students in her school. But there was something different about her. She had no arms.

When Rose was just an infant, a pig ate both of her arms. Her mother was so repulsed, she took baby Rose a few miles outside the village and just left her by the side of the road. She was later adopted by a Christian couple who placed her in a Christian school.

Though Rose was lacking something the other students had, you couldn't tell it from her smile. She laughed heartily and personified contentment.

All of us go through tough times. Everyone experiences problems and trials. Often, we spend time asking why this has happened or analyzing the problem. The issue really isn't *what* we experience . . . it's *how* we handle it that matters.

My high school youth minister once said, "The king of my mountains must also be the lord of my valleys." In other words, it's not enough to serve God and live a holy life when things are going great. Anyone can do that. It's learning to praise Him when we don't understand what's going on around us that shouts volumes to the non-Christians who watch our lifestyle.

You probably know someone who has had more than their share of problems, yet they remain spiritually strong. You may also know someone (like the examples listed earlier) who went through a tough time and blamed God. In every hardship, that's exactly what will always happen: We will either use the problem to grow stronger, or we will allow it to defeat us.

What makes the difference? Why do some people blossom during trials and others blow up?

It's all in how you look at it. When I think of someone who

had a tough time and still maintained his perspective, I think of Job. Despite major problems, Job remained faithful.

According to the Old Testament book of Job, Job was the wealthiest man in the land of Uz. He was also a very godly man. But talk about problems . . . whew! Check out his assets: He owned seven thousand sheep, three thousand camels, five hundred teams of oxen, five hundred female donkeys, and he employed several servants.

When disaster struck, he lost *all* of his animals, his servants, his children, and even his wife. To make matters worse, his best friends weren't even supportive.

But through it all, Job remained faithful to God. He valued his relationship with God and stood firm in his beliefs. In the end? God rewarded him with more than he'd started with!

BEAR STRATEGY

So, let's come up with a plan. Next time you're faced with a "bear attack"—a problem, trial, or tough time—think through the following strategy:

1. Examine yourself. Stop and think. Are you doing anything to attract a bear? Are you eating a peanut butter and jelly sandwich out in the open? If so, bears are going to come your way.

In other words, are you doing anything to attract trouble? Casey's parents were out of town for the day. He slept late on Saturday morning and then rented a few videos. By evening something was wrong. Very wrong. He called his youth pastor and screamed, "There are demons inside my house!" Jim rushed to his home and began praying. After a long while, Casey finally felt at peace. Jim then posed a very important question.

"Casey, what have you been doing all day?"

"I've been watching *The Exorcist,* the *Friday the 13th* movies, and a bunch of other stuff."

Major clue: If you're watching R-rated videos and wondering why you're having trouble with your thought life, or sensing evil around you, put the pieces together—you're inviting it.

Jesus is referred to as the Great Physician. Ask Him to give you a spiritual examination and bring to your mind anything you might be doing to attract trouble.

2. Put on the armor. God has provided protection for your attack. Take advantage of that. Make good use of His armor. (Check out Ephesians 6:11–17 for the specifics.)

When he lists the items in the Christian's armor, Paul mentions several different pieces, one of which is the belt of truth. This was a key section of armor because all the other pieces connected to the belt. If you didn't have the belt, you couldn't have the rest of the armor. It was essential. The belt also covered the private organs of the fighter. Paul chose the belt as TRUTH and as the first piece of armor to put on.

If we respond to God's truth, it enables us to move freely in the power of His Spirit. His truth helps us see ourselves as we really are. (Sneak a peek at John 8:31–32 for more good stuff on truth.) It's important that we know the truth—and more than just head knowledge. God's truth needs to become an *intimate* experience for us.

In the midst of a "bear attack" or when you're right in the middle of a huge problem, ask God to help you see and know the truth about yourself and about the situation.

3. What can I learn from this? Every problem has the potential to help us become stronger. So how about it? Instead of focusing on how difficult it is to go through this tough time, why not ask yourself what you can glean to make you a better person?

Sherry dates often, but can't figure out why her relationships are always short-lived. She fails to learn from her mistakes. Each time she dates a new guy, she falls head over heels. She bakes him cookies, calls him every night, shows up at his house or apartment—and you know what's coming—it only takes about three weeks for the guy to start feeling trapped. So what happens? He breaks up with her.

I've been tempted to say, "Hey, Sherry! Learn from this one. Instead of complaining about how many dating problems you experience, change your thinking, and get something positive out of your next breakup!"

4. I don't gotta be strong—I just gotta plug in. It's not necessarily the strongest who survive a bear attack. Many times the ones who surface to the top of their problems are the ones who are flexible, adaptable, and plugged into a strong resource system.

Remember that TV show "McGuyver"? Little guy, wasn't he? Stack him next to Sylvester Stallone or Arnold Schwarzenegger, and who would you pick to come out on top?

Yet show after show, he continued to prove you don't have to be a "he-man" to be a winner. He was adaptable. He had all these resources. I mean this guy could make a bomb out of a chewing gum wrapper! It was incredible. He always escaped. Always came out on top.

Works the same way with us. If we're not flexible, our problems will eat us alive. We don't have to be physically strong or beautifully built to survive a bear attack. If we're plugged into the Master's resources, however, we'll find He has a million different ways to help us handle our trials.

5. Know that it will pass. Ever read the children's book *Where the Wild Things Are*? It's one of my favorites. In the story, Max wore a wolf suit to supper one evening and was sassy to his mom, so he was sent to bed without any supper. While Max was in his room, a forest grew and he sailed into another world, the world of "wild things." He fought off enemies and eventually became king of the wild things. After ruling for years and years, he finally decided to sail back to his own home where he was loved and cared for. And when he opened his eyes, his supper was next to his bed. And it was still hot.

Though it seemed like forever, Max actually only day-dreamed for about three minutes. It was a short enough time span for his supper to still be hot. And though it often seems like our problems are lasting forever, they WILL come to an end. We won't always be fighting bears.

STUFF YOU DON'T HAVE TO PRAY ABOUT

Fact of life: Everyone has problems. You're not the exception. Though God wants your happiness even more than *you* do, He never promised an easy life. He *did* promise never to leave us and that we wouldn't face anything stronger than we could bear with His help.

Again, the issue is not that you're under attack. Rather, it's how you handle the attack. Will you be a survivor or a victim?

No need to spend time praying for a problem-free, easy life. Sometimes God doesn't fix broken things but gives us power to overcome the brokenness.

STUFF YOU SHOULD PRAY ABOUT

In every trial you will either be overcome or you will overcome. To mature into a disciple whose faith remains rock-solid in the midst of confusion, trials, attacks, and major tough times, pray for:

1. A strong defense. Ever watch professional baseball players on television? Even before the pitcher steps up to the mound, he's tossing and catching balls on the sidelines. As he approaches his position on the mound, he bends over and picks up a handful of dirt and rubs it between his hands. He adjusts his hat, focuses his attention on the batter, pulls back his glove, hurls the ball, and assumes a defensive position. If the ball is slugged in his direction, he's ready for it. He's on the defense.

Christ want us to live on the defense, too! He wants us to be on our toes—watching, alert, ready to fight evil. Assume your

Bible is your baseball glove. It's what you'll use for protection against Satan's deadly arrows that are being slugged your way. Don't stand with your glove between your knees. Use the Word of God to help you be on the defense in your relationship with Him. Christianity isn't passive—it's active!

Ammunition: 1 Peter 5:8 and Ephesians 6:12 tell you who to expect an attack from. And to live and act *defensively*, what should you be wearing? (Check out Ephesians 6:11, 13–17 for your wardrobe.)

2. Insight as to whether you're attracting a problem. Ask God to search your life and show you anything you might be doing to cause a stumbling block in your own life.

Ammunition: Check out Romans 6:16–17. What can you choose? God will equip you with the power you need to overcome the temptation to do wrong.

What does God promise in 1 Corinthians 10:13–14? If you place your trust in Christ, He will show you how to avoid doing something to attract a problem.

3. Perseverance. No matter what comes your way, you want to steadily march on, right? That's what catches the attention of your non-Christian friends. *That's* what makes them want what you have.

Ammunition: Read 2 Thessalonians 3:5 in the NIV. What does God want to direct you toward? And check out Hebrews 10:36. According to this passage, why is perseverance so important? Try memorizing 1 Peter 5:9–11. What promise is given?

4. Growth. Again, don't be like my friend Sherry who never learns from her dating mistakes. Be willing to grow in strength and character each time you face a battle.

Ammunition: James 1:2–4. What is promised you for not trying to squirm out of your problems? According to 1 Peter 1:7, why do we even have trials?

5. Victory. Again, God wants your spiritual success even more than you do. Strive to remember that no matter how difficult the situation gets, it won't be more than you can handle.

Ammunition: 2 Corinthians 4:7–9. What stands out to you personally in these verses? Claim it. Then live your life by it!

> Jesus, I confess that many times I lose complete perspective when I'm going through a tough time. I tend to blame those around me and sometimes even question Your love for me. Help me, instead, to look for how I can benefit from hard times. Teach me to use my trials to produce character and integrity.
>
> And thanks, Father, for paying such a high price for my spiritual victory. No matter how dark my world may seem, help me to remember that as long as You are Lord, I have a hope and a future. Amen.

STUFF TO GROW ON #6

MORE STUFF YOU DON'T HAVE TO PRAY ABOUT

You don't have to spend time asking God if you should:

- Be kind.
- Break the speed limit.
- Respect those in authority whether you agree with them or not.
- Be a man/woman of your word. (If you commit to something, follow through.)
- Give to those in need.
- Attend church regularly.
- Take your schoolwork seriously.
- Be nice to animals.
- Reach out to new kids.
- Be loving toward old people.
- Monitor what you watch on TV.

- Use your money wisely.
- Value people.
- Take care of your possessions.
- Use your talents.

12

GOD'S LOOKING FOR TALKERS

Throughout history, God has used ordinary people to impact their world. *Ordinary* people. People with only one or two talents. People like you and me, who sometimes get angry and lonely and hate practicing the piano.

And through these ordinary, everyday people, God has defeated armies, turned a small group of slaves into a great nation, split seas, healed the sick, and melted the hardened hearts of sinners.

All this and more through people who were *willing to be used by Him*. THAT'S the key to having an impact for God in the world. Are you willing? Would you dare to tell someone else about your faith? Daniel did. Moses dared. And Abraham. So did Noah, Enoch, Abel, Sarah, Jacob, Joshua, Jonah. Well . . . Jonah was a different story. Yeah, he told all right. But he sure wasn't excited about it. He just wasn't a happy camper. You remember the story, don't you? Maybe we'd better take a quick peek . . . just in case.

Let's set the scene:

Place: Nineveh. Old city. Population: approximately 120,000 with more people constantly moving in. Fastest-growing city of its time.

Problem: City with a bad rep. Quickly becoming more and more wicked. (You've heard of other wicked places in the Bible: Sodom, Gomorrah, and the whole world in Noah's time!)

Solution: Destroy the city. Hmmm. Has to be a better plan. Sure would be a tragedy for 120,000 people to die without ever knowing they could have received forgiveness for their sins and lived a better life.

Better Solution: Have someone tell them about God.

Newly Recruited Be-the-One-Spokesman: Jonah.

Complication: Jonah didn't wanna "be the one." Too selfish. Too comfortable watching TV.

Further Complication: God commanded him to "be the one." (Repeat after me: *When God speaks, it makes sense to obey.*)

What Happened: Jonah complained that Nineveh was too far. Also a little too wild. Yep, he'd heard of their bad rep and didn't want to spoil his good rep by hanging around those people. Jonah wanted God to destroy them! Thought they deserved it.

(Hmmm. Sounds like he needed an attitude check.)

So he went to a travel agent and bought a ticket for a cruise, thinking if he ran far enough away, sooner or later God would just forget the whole thing.

This was no *Love Boat*. He set sail on the *Pacific Princess* which was full of superstitious sailors. Instead of trying to share his faith with them, he went to the bottom of the ship to catch some Z's. (All that running from God had worn him out!)

But God knew exactly where Jonah was. (He always knows where we are too.) And He allowed a terrible storm to erupt at sea. It was such a nightmare than even those rough, macho sailors (who were professional seamen) were frightened.

They knew Jonah was a religious man. (They saw him wearing his "See You at the Pole" ID bracelet and noticed his Bible stacked on top of his luggage.) So they woke him up and begged him to pray for their safety.

Pray for *them?* Jonah didn't feel like praying for anyone! His conscience bothered him too much. The ship continued to weave back and forth, back and forth, back and . . . (Are you getting seasick yet?) Fifteen-foot waves emptied themselves on board. Mighty scary times.

Even though Jonah was acting like a jerk, he still had one thing going for him. *He was honest.* So he straightened his back and 'fessed up. "I'm the reason for this storm," he volunteered.

Quiz Time: How did the sailors respond?

A. Said, "Let's talk about your feelings of guilt."

B. Asked if Jonah knew how to jet ski.

C. Put their arms around him and said, "Ah, Jonah. Don't be so hard on yourself."

D. Tossed him overboard.

ANSWER: He was HISTORY as far as the sailors were concerned! They tossed their new passenger right over the side of the ship.

IT'S NOT OVER YET!

But God wasn't finished with Jonah just yet. (You already know this part of the story because you've heard it since you were in kindergarten.) The Lord sent a huge fish (about the size of a mammoth whale, which is probably the size of a football field . . . well, *maybe*) to swallow Jonah.

Jonah spent three days and three nights in his new home. Lots of fish 'n' chips for dinner! Talk about boring—what can you do in the belly of a whale? (1) Untangle the intestines, then measure them; (2) backstroke through the stomach juices; (3) taste the gastric acids; (4) chip off the ol' bone marrow; (5) make seaweed soup for breakfast; (6) alphabetize all the stuff a whale eats—like license plates, people, shoes, octopi, school buses; (7) think.

Jonah chose the last one. He thought. And thought. And thought some more. He realized his back was against a wall. Listen to what he says in Jonah 2:7: "When I had lost all hope, I turned my thoughts once more to the Lord" (TLB).

Typical, huh? When we've lost all hope, then we turn to the Lord. Things could have been so much better if Jonah had just obeyed in the first place! But Jonah tried to do things his own way and ended up inside the digestive system of a giant fish.

Gag! (Literally.) God caused the fish to gag, and Jonah came out in its vomit. Not a pretty picture, is it? But Jonah finally got the point that he couldn't escape God, and this time he went straight to Nineveh and began preaching. He told the people if they didn't turn from their wicked ways, the Lord would destroy their city in forty days.

He still needed an attitude check, though, because when the people got interested enough to stop and listen, Jonah secretly wished they'd continue on their merry way and die in sin.

But the people were intrigued. They never realized there was an all-powerful God who cared about how they lived. (Your friends will be intrigued, too, when you begin sharing your faith.) The Ninevites prayed, asked God to forgive their sins, turned from their wicked ways, and cleaned up their act.

The king even gave his life to God, then ordered everyone else to do the same. (Wow! *That's* throwing your power around.)

Jonah took his lousy attitude and waited underneath a shade tree outside the city gates hoping, wishing, and pleading for God to burn down the city with fire from heaven. But God didn't. He didn't need to. The mission had been successful. The citizens of Nineveh were now believers.

So what did Jonah do? Praise God for using him? Nope. He threw a temper tantrum. "This is exactly what I thought you'd do, Lord, when I was in my own country and you first told me to come here. That's why I ran away to Tarshish. For I knew you were a gracious God, merciful, slow to get angry, and full of kindness; I knew how easily you could cancel your plans for destroying these people. Please kill me, Lord. I'd rather be dead than alive [when nothing that I told them happens]" (Jonah 4:2–3, TLB).

Wowsers! Attitude check, Jonah. Why are you so concerned about what people are going to think of you, rather than being excited that God used you to make a difference in thousands of lives?

"Then the Lord said, 'Is it right to be angry about this?'" (Jonah 4:4, TLB).

MAJOR ATTITUDE CHECK!

Jonah just continued to sit . . . outside . . . in the sun . . . underneath a shade tree . . . and sulked. Then a worm started chewing on the shade tree, and it withered. So Jonah began complaining about that! (Some people never learn.)

Without the shade tree, he got a severe sunburn and was so miserable and physically sick he pleaded with God to let him die:

"Death is better than this!"

And God said to Jonah, "Is it right for you to be angry because the plant died?"

"Yes," Jonah said, "it is; it is right for me to be angry enough to die!" (Jonah 4:8–9, TLB)

Maybe God should have granted his wish right then, but He continued to deal with him. There was still an important lesson for Jonah to learn. God wasn't finished with him yet.

"Then the Lord said, 'You feel sorry for yourself when your shelter is destroyed, though you did no work to put it there, . . . Why shouldn't I feel sorry for a great city like Nineveh with its 120,000 people in utter spiritual darkness?' " (Jonah 4:10–11, TLB)

Hits you between the eyes, doesn't it? (God has a way of doing that sometimes.) People in your school are in utter spiritual darkness. Yet all you can think of is complaining about petty, unimportant things.

Your friends are dying! *What could be more important than sharing God with them?* What could possibly be as high a priority as "being the one" to give them God's message of hope and salvation?

I like Isaiah's attitude. "Then I heard the Lord asking, 'Whom shall I send as a messenger to my people? Who will go?'

"And I said, 'Lord, I'll go! Send me' " (Isaiah 6:8, TLB).

Now THAT'S an attitude God is pleased with!

So . . . will you tell?[1]

STUFF YOU DON'T HAVE TO PRAY ABOUT

God has made it clear: Anyone who doesn't know Him personally is dying. Will YOU dare to share your faith with those around you?

"Well . . . I'll pray about it."

WHY? Do you really need to spend time praying about something God has already told you to do? I don't think so.

STUFF YOU SHOULD PRAY ABOUT

God has gifted each of us with doing certain things well. He wants you to share your faith by using the gifts He's placed within you. In other words, He created you just the way you are *on purpose.* If you're outgoing and love to be in front of people, He'll use that for HIS glory.

If you don't like crowds and would much rather be with one or two close friends, He'll use that for HIS glory. The key is for you to use what He's blessed you with in spreading His message to those around you.

So instead of praying about whether you should tell your friends about Christ, pray instead for God to help you:

1. Live your calling. Do you enjoy having people over? Planning parties? Counseling others? Working behind the scenes? Being in the limelight? Use the skills and abilities He's given you to make an impact for Him.

Ammunition: Read Romans 12:6–8. See anything in this passage that sounds like one of your gifts? And check out 1 Corinthians 12:22. What does this tell you about the variety of God's people? Now look at 1 Corinthians 12:27–31. What are your gifts?

2. Live the light. When Jesus Christ reigns in your life, you have the greatest gift in the entire world. Think about it: You walk hand in hand with the Creator of the universe every single day. You're on a first-name basis with GOD! That's powerful. Why keep it to yourself? Brag a little . . . let others know who you know.

Ammunition: What does Matthew 5:13–14 have to say about sharing your best friend with others? How can your relationship with Christ affect those around you?

3. Live your faith. Your LIFE is even more important than your WORDS. You can talk about God all you want . . . but if your life doesn't match what you're saying, it won't do any good.

What attracts others to Christ? It's not really a church building, or a fun, organized program. It's the *people.* They see something different in the life of an on-fire Christian, and they want what that person has.

When a non-Christian is attracted to you, it will be because of your lifestyle. It will be because you're allowing the Holy Spirit to reflect Christ through you. When someone does ask you about your faith, be ready to share your beliefs.

Ammunition: Read John 15:26–27. Who will help you tell others about the Lord? Check out 2 Timothy 4:1–2. According to these verses, when is it the right time to share your faith?

Dear Lord, I WANT to tell others about You. I get nervous, though. And I feel weird inside. Fill me with Your peace and Your presence. As I get to know people better, help me to begin sharing You in daily, ordinary ways.

I don't want to keep my gift of eternal life a secret. I want my friends in heaven with us! I'll trust You to let me know when the opportunity is right. Thanks, Father. Amen.

Notes

1. *Reprinted with permission from* Keeping Your Cool While Sharing Your Faith *by Greg Johnson and Susie Shellenberger, Tyndale Publishing. Copyright 1993.*

13

WHAT KIND OF PERSON DOES GOD CHOOSE?

The Bible mentions a man named Goliath. Most of us know one thing about him—he was a giant. But I'd like to share some inside information with you.

First of all, he stood about nine feet tall in his stocking feet. His throat was so big, he could swallow a Big Mac, large fries, cherry pie, and large Coke all at once!

He never wore deodorant. It took an entire can of spray for each underarm, and he realized quickly how expensive *that* could get!

No one wanted to be his locker partner at school because every time he "tossed" his books onto the shelf, the entire locker collapsed. The school administration was afraid to give Goliath the repair bill, so his partner always got stuck with having to ace the cost of defacing school property.

Biology class was horrendous. When they dissected frogs, Goliath, with knife in hand, not only cut through the left and right aorta of his frog—but put his knife right through the table as well.

He was a nightmare of a man. So what in the world was twelve-year-old David thinking when he thought he could handle this scary-berry mess of a giant?

David had a talent. He was good with a slingshot. And at a very early age, he committed everything in his life to God. At this early age, he just had one skill. But he gave his skill to God and expected Him to use it. You see, it really doesn't matter how much ability we have. What matters is if we have *availability*.

It was no accident that David killed Goliath with a slingshot. It was not fate, and it was certainly no coincidence. David had practiced day after day for years with his slingshot. He had given his talent to God, and on a daily basis made that talent consistently available. God had spent a LIFETIME preparing David for this giant. It wasn't luck that made David the winner; it was the fact that he was available for God to use.

What has God been preparing *you* for? I don't know what giant you may be facing right now. I don't know what giants will cross your path next week or two years from now. But I do know this: If you'll commit everything in your life to God and make yourself available to Him, He'll equip you with everything you need to handle the giants that cross your path.

All through the Bible, God uses people we would never choose for leaders. God has used ordinary people with little ability to accomplish fantastic tasks. Take Moses, for example. THERE'S a man we wouldn't have chosen!

Moses had a speaking problem. Maybe he had a lisp, and when he spoke it sounded as if he had a mouth full of rocks. It was hard to understand him. And sometimes he stuttered, and it took too much effort to try to decipher his unorganized thoughts. *This* was the man God chose to lead His people out of captivity?

Moses certainly wasn't chosen for his ability. He had nothing going for him. Whenever Hollywood produces a movie about Moses, they always give the part to some he-man with fake whiskers glued onto his face. The truth is, Moses may have looked a lot more like Herman the vacuum cleaner salesman than a weight-lifting monster. But God chose Moses. And He blessed him, protected him, guided him, and showed him first-hand what could happen when he committed *everything* to the Lord.

Now Moses didn't have any ability to speak of . . . but he did have something. Moses had a walking cane. He placed great importance on this rod. It was the only material possession he owned. During the forty years in the desert, God asked for control of even Moses' walking cane.

Moses wasn't sure he wanted to do that at first: "But God! This walking cane is all that I have! It's my security. I need it to guide me through the wilderness. Don't forget, I'm doing your work here. I need a walking stick."

But God continued to deal with Moses until he was willing to be available. When Moses finally committed his material possession to God, he watched in amazement as the Lord took an ordinary piece of wood and transformed it into a dynamic instrument full of power. The rod of Moses became the rod of God, splitting entire rivers in two and commanding water from dry rocks.

IMAGINE THIS

God, too, wants to do exciting things in all of our lives. All we have to do is let Him.

One day Jesus was speaking to over 5,000 people. It must have been Labor Day because nothing was open. Long John Silver's, McDonald's, and even Taco Bell were all closed. He quickly called a board of disciples meeting. "How are we going to feed all these people?" Jesus asked His main men. (He knew exactly where the food would come from, but He wanted to see if the disciples had done their homework.)

The Big Twelve quickly began estimating the size of the crowd. "Let's see . . . there's Mr. Simpkins—we all know how much HE eats! And the Jones family has at least a hundred in it. Then there's the Rodriguez triplets and the Baptist Youth Choir . . . hmmm, there must be over 5,000 people here. Sorry, Jesus.

Can't be done. It would take over a year's wages to feed this crowd. No can do."

Andrew, however, had made friends with a small boy in the crowd who had offered to share his sack lunch. "There's this boy in the crowd—doesn't have much, but he's willing to share the little that he does have." So Jesus motioned for the small boy to come forward. The child gave Christ his mashed fish and crumpled pieces of bread, watching in wonder and amazement as Jesus placed His hands over the food and blessed it.

The boy had never seen anything like it in his life. The bread just kept on coming. Where was it coming from? Jesus had no sleeves; it was simply coming from His hands. It was incredible! The boy's eyes grew wild with excitement.

The feeding of the 5,000 will always be a miracle to remember. But an even greater miracle occurred as well. And that's the fact that a little boy gave Jesus *all that he had*. The little boy was available.

ABILITY OR AVAILABILITY?

Again, God doesn't care about how much or how little ability you have. God cares about your *availability*.

What happened when a twelve-year-old boy gave all he had to God? God took what little he had to offer and killed a giant. God changed the lives of David's people, all because he was available. What happened when one man gave his prayer life to God? God rescued an entire nation through one man's availability.

What happened when a man with no ability and no support gave God everything he had? God took an ordinary piece of wood and transformed it into an instrument of dynamic power. Through one man's availability, God took a small band of slaves and made them into a great nation.

What happened when a small boy gave Jesus Christ everything? A miracle was recorded in the Gospels, spiritually feeding infinitely more than the original 5,000.

What kind of person does God choose to use? Not necessarily the one with the ability but *always* the one with availability.

STUFF YOU DON'T HAVE TO PRAY ABOUT

Settled: God wants you to be available for Him. Period. So, you don't need to plead "Lord, if I could only play volleyball like Shaun. Or if You could just make me sing like Amy Grant, play piano like Michael W. Smith or write songs like Steven Curtis Chapman. Or if I could just be more outgoing, or get the lead in the school play. But I could never make an impact for You, because I'm just not _____ enough."

Instead, shift your focus to a positive prayer life. (We'll talk about how in just a second, okay?)

Since God cares more about your availability than He does your ability, let's stop thinking and praying about all you can't do or the things you wish you could do, and pray instead, about something much more important.

STUFF YOU SHOULD PRAY ABOUT

When you first gave your life to Christ, you were being available. Make your commitment to availability an ongoing matter of prayer. In fact, there's nothing more important for you to pray about than your availability. Your availability to God also includes your time, talent, future, commitment level—it involves everything. So pray specifically for the following:

1. To have a tender heart. People who allow their hearts to harden cannot remain available. It's only by remaining soft-hearted and open to the leading of the Holy Spirit that we can live out our availability.

Ammunition: Philippians 2:1. What does this particular passage say about tenderness?

2. To be used by God in a mighty way. The sky's the limit when God has all of you. Think about it. When you have all of God and He has all of you, there's absolutely nothing He can't accomplish.

Ammunition: Malachi 3:10. What does God promise He will do if you'll simply be faithful to His commands?

Dear Jesus, more than anything in the world, I want to be available to You. I ask that You begin now using me to make a positive and mighty impact on others.

I'm sorry I sometimes slip into a negative mindset about all the stuff I can't do and all the things I wish I were better at. Help me instead to focus on everything You can and will do through me if I'll remain consistently available to Your leading. I love You, Father. Amen.

STUFF TO GROW ON #7

MORE STUFF YOU DON'T HAVE TO PRAY ABOUT

You don't have to spend time praying about whether or not you should:

- Establish healthy friendships.

- Give to missions.

- Develop a strong prayer life.

- Avoid littering.

- Memorize Scripture.

- Pay your bills on time.

- Refuse to gossip.

- Take your responsibility as a citizen seriously (voting when you're of age, being informed of current events, etc.).

- Pay close attention during church.

- Avoid prejudice.
- Take care of God's earth.
- Articulate *what* you believe and *why* you believe it.
- Deepen your relationship with Christ.
- Dress modestly.
- Encourage your pastor.

14

WHERE'S YOUR HEAD?

Twelve people changed the world. They altered the course of history and shattered the face of reality. These twelve people were Christ's disciples. They were just like you. They worried a lot. They were scared. They struggled with peer pressure. They were insecure. Sometimes they worried about their looks. But they changed the world.

They were guys you could've bumped into at the mall. You might have seen them trying on a pair of Reeboks or buying a baked potato with the works at the food court. They were just like you. Yet they changed the world!

How did twelve ordinary men who made tons of mistakes accomplish such an incredible task? They didn't have a youth group to support them. They'd never been on a teen missions trip or had experience standing at their school flagpole in prayer. They'd never even heard a missionary speaker. Yet they changed the world.

I'm convinced twelve ordinary people like you and me were able to turn the world upside down, no, right side up because they had a solid mindset. They refused to be deterred. They realized what went into their minds would determine what they set their minds on.

Since God created our minds, He knows what a powerful thing the mind is. Proverbs 4:23 says: "Be careful what you think—your life is shaped by your thoughts" (TEV).

My *life* is shaped by my thoughts? Whew. That's quite a statement. If that's true (and I choose to believe God's Word is true), then my thinking affects everything I do. The way I dress, the friends I hang out with, the things I do to get a laugh, how I spend my time, what I do with my money . . . everything is influenced and determined by what goes on in my head.

Ralph Waldo Emerson (he's that guy you were supposed to study in English class) said: "A man is what he thinks about all day long." A man is whatever he thinks about? Wow. I better watch what's going on with my thought life, huh?

Mark Anthony (he's that guy you were supposed to study in history class) said: "Change your thoughts—change your life!"

Again, if this is true, then the mind has a lot of power. What we THINK about is going to make a difference in how we live our lives. To a degree, we can say that it's our thinking that makes us who and what we are. That's why Paul (he's that guy you were supposed to study in Sunday School) said: "Fix your thoughts on what is true and good and right" (Philippians 4:8, TLB).

What is your mind set on? Again, God is searching for disciples who will set their minds on Christ; He's looking for disciples who refuse to be swayed by the world's opinions and beliefs.

According to Proverbs 4:23, our lifestyle is shaped by our thoughts. Psychologists tell us that our thoughts produce behavior. So . . . what are you thinking about?

THE MIND IS A POWERFUL THING

Even though she encouraged us to attend every practice, my college tennis coach knew we would miss some. One day she said, "If you have to miss, at least practice your serve in your mind. See yourself tossing the ball at just the right height. Picture bringing back your racket and coming in with a perfect follow-through."

We all realized, of course, we had to pour a lot more than thoughts into developing a good serve, but we also learned that thinking about doing it right actually helped our performance.

It wasn't a "name it and claim it" strategy, but rather a time of working it out in our minds and striving to match our behavior to the picture in our thoughts.

Christ wants to saturate our minds with Himself. If our thoughts are filled with Him, and with positive, holy, good things, our behavior will be affected. Why is this so important? Because it's disciples with a godly mindset who will continue to change the world. And if we have a solid, godly mindset, we'll be less swayed by the world's views.

New Agers know how important our thinking is. They'll say all you have to do is think about something long enough, and it's yours. Want a new car? Visualize it. In a matter of time, you'll be in the drivers seat. Want more power? Imagine it's yours, and you'll have it.

This line of thinking is not scriptural. But a Christian whose mind is not settled is easy prey for the New Age roundup. One day when I was teaching speech class, a student gave an informative oral presentation on his personal beliefs. Larry stood confidently in front of the class and claimed that Jesus Christ was no more the Son of God than he was.

He went on to say that all of us are on a spiritual journey. "There are actually several ways to reach heaven," he said. "Some of you have chosen Christianity. That's one way. Others have chosen Buddha. I am on a personal journey to becoming my own god. It's simply a matter of time before I have more power."

Then he talked about how God was everywhere. "He doesn't just live inside you," Larry said. "He's in the floor I stand on, and inside my note cards—even in your desks. So, in a sense, all these things are God."

He explained his crystal. "I draw and receive energy from it," he said. "Since God is a part of this crystal—and since God is power and energy—I have access to that when I have my crystal."

Larry was an intelligent young man. Good-looking. Popular. Sharp. Confident. Articulate. Even convincing. I wondered if the few Christians I did have in class were being swayed or if their minds were set SOLIDLY on Jesus Christ.

Students listened intently as he continued . . . many of them never knowing Larry was propagandizing them with New Age beliefs.

New Age thinking is not to be taken lightly. It's sweeping our nation like a quickly-growing fire and is one of the fastest growing beliefs in the world right now.

Many school systems have incorporated New Age techniques in their curriculum. New Age books are selling rapidly. Channelers, astral projection, tarot cards, crystals, and even some "angel" paraphernalia are all a part of the New Age movement.

This is not a small club or a coastal fad. It involves people from all walks of life. Shirley MacLaine has sold more than eight million copies of her New Age book, *Out on a Limb*, and has made a prime-time television movie on its content.

New Age bookstores have doubled recently. There are now over 2,500 nationwide. Bantam books reports that New Age book titles have increased over ten times in ten years. The Gallop Poll reports that 25 percent of people in the United States believe in some form of reincarnation.

Did you know there are more than one thousand channelers in Los Angeles alone? For a fee, they will supposedly get you in touch with someone who has died. New Age merchandising is slick. The vocabulary is seductive with phrases like "cosmic harmony" and "self-realization."

We need to pierce through all this glamour and realize through the Word of God that this is a counterfeit, false religion. It's nothing more than hungry people searching for God's truth. We expect those who don't know Christ to fall for that stuff. But sadly enough, they're not the only ones who are being swept up in New Age philosophies. Again, Christians whose minds are not focused completely on Christ—whose thoughts are not saturated with God Himself—are prime game for the world's belief system.

THAT'S NOT ALL!

The dangerous part of New Age thinking is that if we're all on the pathway to becoming gods, then it really doesn't matter if we sin. Larry stood in front of my speech class and said, "I'm not concerned with what you would label right and wrong. If I do something wrong," he said, "it's simply because I need awareness of that action during this lifetime. For instance, if I kill someone, I'm not going to worry about it. It simply means that, for a reason I'll probably never understand, I needed to know what it would feel like to take a life or spend years behind bars."

Larry believed he was a god. I'm told one of the climactic moments in Shirley MacLaine's movie is a scene in which she's running down a beach screaming, "I am God! I am God—I have finally gained my awareness of my goodness!"

Well, the frightening thing about *that* is once you've rationalized yourself into believing you're God, you'll rationalize yourself into believing that you can:

- call your own shots
- create your own logic
- plan your own life
- make your own rules
- save your own soul
- determine your own destiny
- do your own thing

135

New Age is full of dangerous philosophies and frightening beliefs. Quite bluntly, its doctrine will lead you straight to hell.

So, again . . . what's your mind set on? If not planted firmly on God and His Word, you're easy prey for New Age beliefs. Know WHAT you believe and WHY. Practice being able to articulate your faith. God not only wants to live in your heart—He wants to saturate your thinking . . . to possess your entire life.

THE AUTHOR OF NEW AGE

The same one who's at the heart of the New Age movement is the same one who's at the heart of witchcraft and the same one who wants your mind to be set on the world instead of Christ. You guessed it—the author of all this deceit and confusion is Satan.

I met Jill at a retreat I was speaking at. She told me she was involved in a few New Age teachings. She was also "into" drugs, witchcraft, sexual relationships, and had received an abortion just hours before coming on this church retreat.

After talking and praying with Jill but not getting through, I realized demons were hindering her prayers. Satan had literally blocked her prayer line to God.

Eight youth ministers and I prayed with Jill from 10:00 P.M. to 6:00 A.M., and watched in amazement as demons were cast out of her. Between those long hours, we consistently led her in a prayer of salvation.

It was the most frightening experience I've ever encountered. I watched in horror as Satan threw her to the ground and screamed through her voice. Her body twisted and convulsed with hatred from hell.

Satan glared through her eyes and hissed, "She's mine!"

Why? How did this happen to a girl raised in a Christian home? Her dad had even been a pastor. What went wrong? Though Jill had never verbally invited Satan to invade her life, by her sinful lifestyle she had willingly opened the doorway to accepting the beliefs of the world.

At one time she had made a half-hearted commitment to God. But she'd never *set her mind* firmly on Jesus Christ. She'd never allowed Him to possess her thinking. She was weak-kneed and wishy-washy. Her thoughts and beliefs vacillated back and forth from church to the world to God to friends to the world to church to . . .

Get the picture? God is looking for disciples with their minds set firmly on Him. Disciples who REFUSE to be swayed or influenced by what's going on around them. Disciples who are grounded in their thinking and who are living out God's Word.

One Single Thing

So what happened to Larry? And Jill? The same Larry who so eloquently presented his New Age beliefs in speech class wasn't even old enough to drive a car. Two months earlier, he had gotten a fourteen-year-old girl pregnant, and two weeks after his speech class debut, he was married.

The marriage lasted three weeks. He dropped out of our school and enrolled in another—still searching for something to fill his mind, still desperately hunting for answers to happiness, meaning, and fulfillment.

And Jill? Her new "commitment" lasted almost six months. It was just a matter of time before she fell right back into her old, sinful lifestyle.

Why? Because the mind is a powerful thing! If we're filling our thoughts with things, ideas, philosophies, and ways of the world, our lifestyle will eventually reflect our thinking.

What does it mean to have a godly mindset? It means we're dedicated to one thing—committed 100 percent. Sold out. Firmly attached to. Completely dedicated. But that *one thing has to be Jesus Christ.*

If our minds are set 100 percent on Jesus Christ, our actions will reflect our thoughts. If our hearts are totally dedicated to God, our lifestyle will echo that commitment.

A few years ago there was a minister in the Nashville area whose actions finally caught up with his thoughts. He pastored a successful church. Everything looked GREAT on the outside. But on the inside, his thoughts were far from being planted firmly on God.

He employed a janitor with a similar physique as his own. The janitor had several tattoos, and of course his facial features were different, but other than that, they were very similar in size and appearance.

The minister took out a $100,000 life insurance policy and decided he wanted to cash in. So he *set his mind* on getting rid of the janitor while making it look like HE was the one who had been killed.

He stabbed the janitor to death, shaved off his tattoos, beheaded him, and finally the minister put his own clothes on the body of the dead employee. It looked as if the minister had been murdered. When his wife tried to cash the insurance policy a few months later, the police put a few clues together, found the minister, and eventually arrested him for the crime.

SO, WHERE'S YOUR HEAD?

The Bible tells us that our sins will find us out. In other words, whatever is on the inside *will eventually come out!* King David knew the power of the mind. That's why he prayed, "Search me, Oh God, and *know my heart*." (Read the entire prayer in Psalm 139.) He knew that God could see inside his heart and his mind, so he pleaded with the Lord to correct his wrong thinking.

King David knew from past experience (Bathsheba) that thoughts eventually lead to actions. Thinking = behavior. That's why he fervently and consistently asked God to monitor his thought life. He wanted his thoughts to be godly.

Randy and I were youth ministers at the same church. He worked with the junior high group, and I had the senior high. One day we were riding in his Jeep and his watch beeped. "What's that, Randy?" I asked. "Do you have an appointment you're late for?"

"No," he replied.

"Well, how come your watch is beeping?" I said.

I'll never forget his response. "I've set it to go off every hour, Susie. I use it as a constant reminder. Every time the alarm sounds, I ask myself, 'What are you thinking about, Randy? What's going on in your mind right now?'"

Hmmm. Godly disciples intent on changing the world *care* about their minds. They determine to set their thoughts on God and *saturate* their thinking with Him.

NOW THAT'S BEING SATURATED!

Years ago, a young Communist broke off his engagement with his Christian fiancée. The girl's pastor sent the letter to Billy Graham. I ran across a copy in Charles Swindoll's book *Quest for Character.* Notice the commitment of this young man.

> We Communists have a high casualty rate. We are the ones who get shot and hung and ridiculed and fired from our jobs and in every other way made as uncomfortable as possible. A certain percentage of us get killed or imprisoned. We live in virtual poverty. We turn back to the party every penny we make above what is absolutely necessary to keep us alive.

> We Communists do not have the time or the money for many movies, or concerts, or T-bone steaks, or decent homes, or new cars. We have been described as fanatics. We ARE fanatics. Our lives are dominated by one great overshadowing factor—the struggle for world communism.

We Communists have a philosophy of life which no amount of money can buy. We have a cause to fight for, a definite purpose in life. We subordinate our petty personal selves into a great movement of humanity; and if our personal lives seem hard or our egos appear to suffer through subordination to the party, then we are adequately compensated by the thought that each of us in his small way is contributing to something new and true and better for mankind.

There is one thing which I am in dead earnest about, and that is the Communist cause. It is my life, my business, my religion, my hobby, my sweetheart, my wife, my mistress, and my bread and meat.

I work at it in the daytime and dream of it at night. Its hold on me grows, not lessens, as time goes on; therefore, I cannot carry on a friendship, a love affair, or even a conversation without relating it to this force which both drives and guides my life.

I evaluate people, looks, ideas and actions according to how they affect the Communist cause, and by their attitude toward it.

I've already been in jail because of my ideals and if necessary, I'm ready to go before a firing squad.[1]

This man's thinking was saturated by communism. How sad that his commitment was to this godless philosophy rather than to the God of the universe. Just think about how you could impact your world for Christ if your commitment to Him was similar to this young man's commitment to communism.

STUFF YOU DON'T HAVE TO PRAY ABOUT

Settled: You don't need to pray about New Age doctrines, smooth-sounding ideas, or what your friends are pushing. God has called YOU to *set your mind* firmly on Him—just like the first disciples who were chosen to follow Him.

God is searching for young men and women with a godly mindset. Disciples who will commit even their thoughts to Him.

STUFF YOU SHOULD PRAY ABOUT

You may be tempted to spend your energy praying about a variety of beliefs that the world is pushing. But God has already made the way to heaven explicitly clear in His Word. Choose, instead, to spend your time praying about:

1. Being a godly disciple among those who aren't. Sometimes it's tough to do what's right when everyone around you is doing the opposite. Again, the KEY is to have a godly mindset. In other words, set your mind on Jesus Christ and refuse to allow other junk to sway you.

Daniel had a godly mindset. And because of that, he was able to live a godly lifestyle—even among those who weren't. Not only did he LIVE a godly life . . . he MAINTAINED his integrity in the midst of a heathen court.

Ammunition: Read Daniel 6:3. What set Daniel apart from everyone else? What will set *you* apart? Check out Isaiah 59:15–16. Sound like your world? What is God calling you to do? How can "standing in the gap" set you apart like it did Daniel?

2. Looking past those around you and focusing on God. If your attention is on what everyone else is doing, your thoughts won't be centered around Christ. Remember Stephen? He was stoned for his beliefs, yet he looked right past his murderers and focused his attention instead on Christ. He had a godly mindset. His mind was set on God and God alone.

Ammunition: Familiarize yourself with Stephen's story. It's found in Acts 6:8–15 and Acts 7:54–60. What effect do you think his actions and reactions had on those around him? If you started focusing *your* attention on God instead of people, what kind of impact could you make?

3. Developing a godly mindset. To establish yourself in holy ways and as a reflection of Christ Himself takes the Holy Spirit living through you, and a commitment on your part to set your mind on God and God alone.

Ammunition: 1 Peter 1:13–15. Ah, go ahead and memorize it. Yeah, it's more than a one-liner, but it'll be worth it to have THIS in your head! As you study this passage, ask yourself why God is calling you to live a holy life. How does your mindset affect your holiness? How do your thoughts affect your behavior?

Then check out Psalm 112:1, 7. Since you're already in the "memorizing mode," you might as well get THIS one in your head too. I like the way it sounds from The Living Bible: "Happy is the man who delights in doing [God's] commands . . . For he is *settled in his mind* that Jehovah will take care of him (italic mine).

What's THAT tell you about mindset?

Dear Jesus, I confess I have trouble with my thought life. Many times it's FAR from godly. But You know my heart. And more than anything, I really DO want to be a reflection of You.

So, Lord, help me to discipline my thoughts to You. When ungodly things enter my mind, help me to immediately turn those over to You. Remind me to ask YOU to fill my mind with good and pure things.

Give me a growing hunger for Your Word, for I realize the more Scripture I put into my mind, the more I can dwell on it during times of temptation.

Jesus, like the twelve early disciples who changed the world, I too, want to impact my world. I know that will never happen, though, if my mind is easily swayed and moved by thoughts, people, and ideas around me.

Help me to DIVE into Your Word—to study it, digest it and LIVE it, so that when I am confronted with smooth-sounding philosophies, I'll remain with my mind set firmly on You and You alone. Amen.

Notes

1. *Charles Swindoll*, The Quest for Character (*Portland, Oreg.: Multnomah Press,* 1987), 166–67

STUFF TO GROW ON #8

If you're wanting to put a SPARK in your devotional life, consider grabbing a teen devotional book. Of course, the Bible is the *ultimate* devotional book. But I've found reading a devotional book in the morning and the Bible in the evenings helps add an additional zing to my quiet times with God.

Here are a few of what's available. Visit your local Christian bookstore for more.

- *Beefin' Up, Tunin' Up* and *Fillin' Up* by Mark Littleton (Three-book series/Multnomah)

- *Energizers* by Nate Adams (Zondervan)

- *Heart to Heart* by Rebecca Lyn Phillips (Thomas Nelson)

- *I Can't. God Can. I Think I'll Let Him: Daily Devotions for Girls* by Jane Cairo, Sheri Curry, Anne Christian Buchanan, and Debra Klingsporn (Thomas Nelson)

- *I'm Bailing as Fast as I Can* by Marilyn Cram Donahue (David C. Cook)

- *In Process, In Focus* by Kim Boyce with Ken Abraham (David C. Cook)

- *Jumper Fables* by Ken Davis and Dave Lambert (Zondervan)

- *Ready for Prime Time: Devotions for Girls* by Andrea and Bill Stephens (Fleming Revell)

- *You Take Over, God. I Can't Handle It: Daily Devotions for Guys* by Kevin J. Brown and Ray Mitsch (Thomas Nelson)

- *YouthWalk* (Zondervan)

15

IT'S TOUGH TO RAISE PARENTS THESE DAYS!

Isaac didn't get married until he was over forty. And he waited another twenty years or so before he had kids. So by the time his children were born, their parents looked like grandparents. Pretty old.

Just so happens that Isaac's wife, Rebekah, gave birth to twin boys. One was born with thick red hair, so they named him Esau (which meant hairy). The other twin was born with his hand on Esau's heel, so they named him Jacob (which meant heel-grabber. Sheesh! What were these parents thinking—naming their kids weird names like that?).

Maybe they weren't thinking at all . . . because when Hairy and Heelgrabber started school, you better believe everyone made big-time fun of them! First of all, their parents looked like grandparents. Second, they had these dorky names.

Right from the start, these two kids were in for a tough time. To make matters even more complicated, Mama and Papa Isaac loved to be involved in their children's lives. So when Hairy and Heelgrabber's teacher asked for a parent volunteer to be homeroom monitor, Mama and Papa took the job.

Whenever the school did anything, they were there. Fund-raising carnivals, talent shows, parent-teacher meetings, you name it. And, of course, all the kids were snickering and saying, "Hey, who brought their grandparents?"

And Hairy and Heelgrabber shyly admitted, "They're ours. They're not our grandparents. They're our parents. See, they didn't get married till really late, and then they waited a while longer to have kids, so . . . well, you get it."

It was tough always having to explain. Well, it got even tougher! The Bible tells us that even though the two boys were twins, they were very different. Hairy loved to play outdoors, and he loved fishing and hunting and generally getting completely dirty. He went camping a lot with Papa Isaac.

Heelgrabber, on the other hand, hated dirt, so he stayed inside most of the time and did stuff with his mama. He loved sewing, cleaning, going to Tupperware parties, and competing in quilting bees.

Now there's an interesting twist to this story. It's called "the birthright." In those days the oldest boy received the birthright—which meant everything that was important in the family went to him. The ranch, the animals, the hired help, the jet ski, the four-wheel drive Jeep—everything. Since Hairy was born about a minute before Heelgrabber, he naturally was in line for the birthright.

When the boys were about sixteen years old, and Isaac was almost deaf and couldn't see very well, he decided it was time to pass on the birthright. So he called Hairy into his room and said, "Son, I don't know how much longer I have to live, but I'm going to bless you and pass on the birthright. Tell you what. Go out and kill a deer, cook my favorite meal, bring it back and we'll share it together as a special father/son celebration."

Not a hard assignment. Hairy had been hunting with his dad hundreds of times. He knew exactly where the deer roamed. And together they had slow-cooked venison over an open camp-fire. He knew just the way Papa liked it seasoned. So he left to fulfill his task.

Meanwhile . . . in the next room, with a glass between her ear and the kitchen wall, Mama Isaac heard everything her husband said. *I don't think it's right,* she murmured to herself, *that just because Hairy's maybe a minute older that he should get the birthright.* She was naturally closer to Heelgrabber since they spent more time together. So she began the scheme of deception.

"Heelgrabber!" she called. "Heelgrabber! Come here!" He put down his pot holder loom and sauntered into the kitchen.

"Heelgrabber, I just heard that your dad is ready to pass on the birthright, and I want you to get it instead of Hairy. So, I tell you what. Let's just pull some frozen venison out of the freezer, nuke it in the microwave, and you take it in to his room. He can hardly see, you know. So he'll think you're Hairy, and he'll give you the birthright." She was really proud of herself for coming up with this plan.

But Heelgrabber was a whiner. "Ah, Mama," he said. "It'll never work."

"Well, why not?" she said.

"Because, well . . . I'm not hairy like my brother, Hairy. And if Dad should hug me or something, he'll feel my silky smooth baby-soft skin, and he'll know immediately I'm not Hairy."

"Oh, all right," she said. "We can take care of that." She yanked and pulled and tugged until she was able to get the goat-hair rug out from underneath the refrigerator. Then she cut the rug in strips and tied it around Heelgrabber's chest and back.

"Okay, that should do it," she announced. "Now, here's the venison. Take it to your dad."

"Ah, Mama," he said. "It'll still never work."

"What now?"

"I don't smell bad, like my brother. Whew! When he comes home from those hunting trips—stand back! Papa'll take one whiff of my Polo cologne, and he'll know immediately I'm not Hairy."

"No problem," she said. "Quick fix." She then dug Hairy's dirtiest, grimiest, smelliest clothes from the dirty clothes hamper and gave them to Heelgrabber. "Here. Put these on," she said.

He did. Then, with the goat-hair rug strapped to his chest and back, Hairy's dirty clothes on, and the venison on a special tray, he walked into his papa's room and began the deception.

"Here, Papa," he said. "Here's your special meal that I've prepared just for you."

Okay, Papa Isaac was almost blind and just about deaf, but he was still a sharp cookie, know what I mean? (Basically, he had his doubts.) So he said, "Come here, my son. Repeat in my ear what you've just said."

Heelgrabber moved in. And as he did, Papa Isaac gave him a big bear hug. *Hmmm. Sure FEELS like Hairy,* he thought. Then he took a quick sniff. *And it sure SMELLS like Hairy. Whew!* That was all the proof he needed.

The two men shared the meal together, and when they were done, Isaac blessed Heelgrabber and gave him the birthright.

Heelgrabber took the dishes (couldn't wait to tidy up the kitchen) and left. At that moment Hairy walked in through the other door with steaming hot venison seasoned just the way Isaac liked it.

"Here, Papa," he said. "Here's your favorite dish. Let's share it together and celebrate the passing on of your blessing."

The Bible tells us that as soon as Isaac heard those words, he knew he'd been deceived. He began to cry. Hairy didn't understand. "Papa, why the tears? This is a joyous occasion! Let's celebrate," he said.

"You don't understand," Isaac said. "I've been deceived."

"What are you talking about, Papa? C'mon. Eat your favorite dish. I've seasoned it with all the things you like best."

"No. Your mother and your brother tricked me. I've already had a meal of venison. And thinking your brother was you, I've already given away the birthright."

"What? How could this happen?"

"I'm sorry, my son. I'm so sorry."

Both men wept bitterly. Then Hairy stormed out of the room, and his mom overheard him say, "I'll get even with my brother if it's the last thing I do."

She quickly went to Heelgrabber and said, "Flee for your life! Your brother is out for revenge, and he won't stop till your blood is on his hands."

Heelgrabber ran far and fast. He went to his Uncle Laban's. It was really far. So far, he'd never even visited there before. It was in an entirely different section of the country.

Hairy, meanwhile, began recruiting an army and supplying them with weapons. It would take several years before he could finally track down Heelgrabber. So, while we're waiting . . . let's just interrupt the story for a minute.

WAIT A SECOND

(If we were watching this on the VCR, we'd just push the pause button. So pretend you've just clicked it.)

Was it right for Mama Isaac to deceive her husband and her son? (This is where you move your head yes or no.) Okay, I can feel it. Some of you are nodding your heads up and down. Good. You're still awake. Next question: Is it ever right to deceive anyone? (Head-shaking time again.) Yep, my computer is starting to wiggle. More of you are nodding up and down.

Okay, maybe you're thinking it wasn't right. Can we just go ahead and make a general consensus here? Let's just say that all of you reading this are saying the same thing (even though some of you aren't). Let's just say, "No, it's not right to deceive. Ever. Anyone." Can we just agree to that?

In fact, let's just go ahead and say it was really big time WRONG for Mama Isaac to do what she did. She BLEW it.

But that's not really the issue. Though what Mama Isaac did was wrong, there's something more at stake. The real issue? We serve a God who can make GOOD things happen out of BAD stuff.

We get so caught up with our "rights," don't we? We get all bent out of shape when he does this, or she does that. And we forget that when we belong to God—*really* belong to Him—like 100 percent committed . . . OUR rights become HIS rights. We give Him everything, remember? Not just our future, our temper, our dating life, but our *rights*, too! If you've really given up having to have your way, and have yielded to His way, then GOD OWNS YOUR RIGHTS.

So, again the real issue here is not who deceived whom, or who did the dirtiest, most rottenest stuff. The real issue is: Will Hairy allow God to make something BEAUTIFUL out of this mess?

But an even more important issue is at stake. It's you. You've probably been deceived and treated rotten a few times too. So, what're you going to do about it? Seek revenge? Explode in anger? Stuff it all inside? Or commit it to God and let Him handle it?

RAISING THE PARENTS

Maybe you've even been hurt by a family member. It's a "given" that parents are going to blow it sometimes, like Mama Isaac did. And she didn't just make a small mistake. She sinned in deceiving her husband and in pulling her son into the sin of deception with her. Maybe your parents will blow it big too.

God never said your parents would be perfect. He also never said that you had to agree with everything they did.

Paragraph break: Wish I didn't have to insert this paragraph here, but I think I need to. Statistics tell us that one out of every four girls are sexually abused by a family member. And one out of every twelve boys are sexually abused by a family member. That breaks my heart.

I know that some of you reading this right now are in an abusive situation. (And if you're not, you know a friend who is.) I have to make this clear: IT'S NOT YOUR FAULT! If you're feeling guilty, it's false guilt. It's not God's will that you be abused.

NOWHERE in the Bible does God contradict Himself. So He's not saying, "Obey your parents" and then expecting you to go home and get abused. I believe if you're in an abusive situation, it's His will that you BREAK the trauma of secrecy—and it *is* a traumatic secret—and tell an adult. An adult whom you trust spiritually.

You need someone to believe you and to believe in you. And if that adult doesn't do anything to help lighten your load, then turn around and find another adult to talk with. It's not God's will that you be abused. Things *can* get better. But unless you dare to tell, you're fighting a battle you will not win.

I know. Some of you are thinking, *Susie, you have absolutely NO IDEA what goes on in my house behind closed doors!*

You're right. I don't. But our God does. And He cries your tears with you. And He feels your hurt. Psalm 34:18 tells us that He's very close to those whose hearts are breaking.

In fact, breaking hearts are His specialty. Will you give Him yours?

REVENGE?

We pick up the story about twenty years later. (Didn't even notice your shoes were a little too tight, did ya?) Hairy and his army have finally caught up with Heelgrabber. (We'll unpause the VCR now and continue with the action.)

Hairy sees his brother up ahead. It's actually about a mile away, but it's flat land and he can see that far. (If you've ever been to Oklahoma or parts of Texas, you know what I'm talking about.) He holds up his arm and halts the army. "Back me up. But I want first blood." So the army stands still, watching, waiting.

Hairy adjusts his weapon belt and continues forward. He's a time bomb just waiting to e-x-p-l-o-d-e! But God's love has been working over the years . . . overtime, double-time, triple-time.

Hairy has a strong wall of hate on the inside of his heart. It's constructed with big bricks that say BITTERNESS, JEALOUSY, ANGER, and REVENGE.

He continues walking . . . seething. And God's love continues to act, to spill out on the inside. Hairy is steamed; God is moved.

"Let me have My way, Hairy," God says.

He spits on the ground, wipes the sweat off his brow and continues forward. "He had no right!"

"But let ME take care of this."

"He ruined EVERYTHING!"

"There's a better way, Hairy."

"How COULD he?"

"I can make something BEAUTIFUL out of this—if you'll let Me."

"It was MY birthright."

"Hairy, let Me work in your heart."

His heart was racing. His hands were trembling. He was under "conviction." (That meant He felt God moving, heard God talking, sensed God's direction, but continued with his own rationalization.)

"MY WAY!"

"No, Hairy. My way. I can make something GOOD out of something BAD."

God's love always wins. Hairy was half a mile away from Heelgrabber. He'd searched for years. God's love began exploding over the thick wall of hate in Hairy's heart. The love knocked over one of the bricks. It was bitterness.

When he was a fourth of a mile away from Heelgrabber, Hairy was shaking so much his weapon belt fell off his waist and tumbled onto the red dirt beneath him.

God's love continued to move. It knocked over another piece of the wall . . . the brick of anger.

Hairy began to cry. When he was five blocks away from Heelgrabber, he was crying so much he couldn't see the road in front of him. Still shaking. Crying. Moved by God's love.

Confused by his reaction. Tired of fighting. Yet uncertain of the immediate future.

Two blocks away, he fell face first into the dirt. And Heelgrabber, knowing it was a risk, walked forward. He stretched out his arms, picked up his brother, and gave him a big bear hug. And two grown men wept like babies in each other's arms.

Family Reunion

And then the remembering began. Flashback time.

Hairy: *Sniff. Sniff.* Heelgrabber, remember when I was eight? And I wanted to be Superman. And we didn't have much money. And we couldn't afford a costume. And you . . . *snort, sniff* . . . were always so good at sewing and stuff. You took down your bedroom curtains and made me a Superman cape. Remember?

Heelgrabber: *Blubber, snortle, sniff.* Yeah, I remember. Mom never did replace those curtains.

Hairy: *Chortle, sniff.*

Heelgrabber: And remember seventh grade? These kids were bullying me for my lunch money, but I wouldn't give it to them because I was hungry. So after school they waited for me and started to beat me up. *Sniff, guffaw, sniff.* Then all of a sudden, you rounded the corner and jumped on 'em! An undercut to the left. A punch in the stomach. YOU took the black eye that should've been MINE. Thanks, Hairy.

Hairy: Yeah. *Sniff. Sniff.* I remember.

Heelgrabber: *Snortle.*

Hairy: And, Heelgrabber, remember our junior year in high school? I was running for class president, and I left my speech on the dresser at home. You cut class right before assembly, rushed home and got it to me just in time for me to present it. Remember? You took detention for me! Thanks, Heelgrabber.

Two grown men. Allowing God to dissolve the bitterness and hate. Two grown men allowing God to make something beautiful out of something dreadful. Something good from something bad.

STUFF YOU DON'T HAVE TO PRAY ABOUT

Settled: There are a few things in this chapter that serve as reminders of stuff you don't need to spend time praying about. Even though they're not perfect, God has given you your parents for a specific reason. Do you really need to spend time praying about whether to love, respect, or honor them? Nope. Sure don't.

And what about those people (maybe people in your family) who have hurt you? Need to spend time praying about whether to forgive them? Nah. Already clear.

And those rights! What about your rights that have been stepped on. How *could* he . . . ah, remember . . . THAT'S not the issue. Thinking about praying for a "get even" moment? Think again. Where are your rights? (Repeat after me: "My rights belong to God.")

STUFF YOU SHOULD PRAY ABOUT

We've covered quite a bit in this chapter, haven't we? So let's start with praying about those rights.

1. Pray for God to have EVERYTHING. God doesn't simply want your rights; He wants you to give Him your lifestyle. When others hurt us, our first reaction (because we're human) is to strike back. After all, we don't understand why someone would want to hurt us, or why we face hard times.

The mark of a growing disciple, though, is to accept without understanding. To allow God to handle the situation for us.

Ammunition: Read Isaiah 26:3. What do you experience when God has EVERYTHING? How will this affect your relationships? Your stress? Your life at school?

And check out Isaiah 26:8–9. Does this passage reflect your earnestness to allow God to rule your life?

2. Pray for comfort. If you're in an abusive situation, or if you've been hurt, you need to be comforted. Imagine yourself sitting in the lap of Jesus with His strong arms around you, taking the hurt away. Will you ask Him to put a Band-Aid across your broken heart?

Ask Him to begin the healing process now that needs to happen in your life. And remember, sometimes it's a process for wounds to heal. That's okay. You have the Great Comforter, remember? He's not leaving you. Lean on Him.

Ammunition: Memorize this one: "O my soul, why be so gloomy and discouraged? Trust in God! I shall again praise him for his wondrous help; he will make me smile again, for he is my God!" (Psalm 43:5, TLB)

And bask in Psalm 84:11. What does God want to do for you? Check out John 14:18. How long will God stay close to you? Keep reading . . . John 14:26. Sound like what you need? Ask! Bonus repeat: John 15:26.

Time for gifts! According to John 14:27, what are you getting?

3. Pray for forgiveness. Are you holding a grudge against someone? Do you harbor a bitter, unforgiving spirit? Then ask God to forgive you for not forgiving those who have hurt you.

The important thing is to be honest. *Pray exactly where you are.* You may not want to forgive. Then start right there.

"Father, I don't even *want* to forgive _____. He (she) has hurt me too bad. But help me to want to want to forgive, because I know your forgiveness toward me hinges on this important matter."

Ammunition: According to Matthew 6:14–15, what do you need to do?

4. Pray for your family. Maybe you have a family member who's not a Christian. Ask God to bring them to Him. Ask Him to give you a genuine spiritual burden for your family.

Ammunition: According to 2 Peter 3:14–16, why is God waiting to return? What does this say about your loved ones who don't yet know Him?

Father, I give my family, my rights, my hurts, myself to You. I don't understand why certain things have happened to me, but I'm going to trust You to make something GOOD happen.

Continue to comfort me, Jesus. I need to feel Your hug. Amen.

16

MIRROR, MIRROR...
WHO DO I SEE?

Cheryl was my prayer partner for two years. I loved praying with her. Well, I loved listening to her pray. It was obvious she was talking to the King of kings. Once in a while, I found myself opening my eyes as she was praying. I caught myself glancing around the room to see if an angel was fluttering close by or a burning bush was about to explode in the corner. In the presence of God—that's how I felt when Cheryl prayed with me. She *possessed* the kingdom of God. And as I watched her life, I saw Jesus.

When Susan was my prayer partner, I loved dialoging with her about the Bible. Like a sponge, she literally soaked up the Word until it saturated her life and started oozing out of her lifestyle. Anytime we discussed anything, she could always draw the parallel to God's Word. She proved the Bible was a modern-day road map for our lives. God didn't just live in her heart—He possessed her whole being. And as I watched her life, I saw Jesus.

CHATTIN' WITH CARMAN

When I did an interview with contemporary Christian artist Carman for a *Brio* magazine article, I couldn't help but notice his intensity about his relationship with Christ. Many artists think before answering questions—but Carman's answers came quick, and they were deep. I started wondering if he'd done so many interviews that he didn't have to really think about his answers and could easily spout off something that sounded good and deep. So I asked, "Are you giving me the same stuff you hand out at every interview? I don't want canned answers."

"No," he said. "Most people don't ask me the questions you're asking. I'm talking from my heart."

Over the course of our dinner, I began to realize that he had such a deep relationship with the Lord, that God was the first thing on his mind. So when asked the questions I was asking, without even thinking he was merely reflecting where he was with God. Everything seemed to relate to his walk with Christ. It was what he thought about, chatted about, read about, LIVED. And yes, I saw Jesus in his life.

WHOSE REFLECTION?

What do people see when they look at your life? Is Jesus shining through? Is your life a mirror of the Lord? In order for Christ to live *through* you, He first must live *in* you. And not just in your heart. He wants to invade your life in an intimate way— that means He wants to be in your thoughts, your actions and reactions, your conversation, your hobbies—He wants to saturate your lifestyle. And when He does? People can't help but notice the difference.

What IS the difference? It's an *intensity*. A *depth*. A *greater level of commitment*. It's *possessing God's kingdom*. It's *being obsessed* with becoming all God calls you to be. These are the marks of a true Christian—someone who loves God with all his or her life and literally wears it every single day when people are watching, and when they aren't.

Realize if you're in this category, you're in the minority. Churches are filled with surface-level, halfway committed disciples. But the Bible calls that level of commitment being "lukewarm." Jesus told us to make up our minds: Be hot or cold.

But living in the middle—riding the fence—having the best of both worlds—being lukewarm, just won't cut it. In fact, Christ said He would spew us from His mouth. In other words, a half-hearted Christian living out a lukewarm commitment will never enter Heaven.

For others to see God in your life, you must DEEPEN your commitment. Again, it means doing what Jesus would do—not just when someone's watching (that's easy!), but doing what He wants you to do when no one's looking. (THAT can be tough!)

CHRISTIANITY COSTS!

I had flown into the Los Angeles airport, had to make a fast connection, and was going to fly on to Oklahoma City. Another passenger who could barely speak English asked me where she could find her connecting flight. I could hardly understand her and knew others probably wouldn't understand her either. I glanced at her ticket, found a display monitor listing the connecting flights and instructed her where to go.

She didn't understand. I pointed her in the right direction, frightened I was going to miss my own flight. She still didn't understand. I finally motioned for her to follow me and rushed through the crowded airport to her departure gate. Once there, she smiled broadly and nodded her head in thanks.

I rushed to catch my plane, and in the process of running, must have dropped my ticket because it was gone when I reached my gate. I barely had enough time to run down to the terminal, purchase another ticket, and hurdle my way back to the gate just in time to claim my seat.

Yeah, I was bummed. I was out of breath, out of money, and out of patience. But somehow, deep down inside, I knew that's exactly what Jesus would have done. He would have taken the lady all the way to her gate, THEN focused on His own needs.

I pulled the seat belt across my waist, shared the crowded armrest with the stranger next to me, and smiled. *Thanks, Lord, for reminding me what my purpose here is all about. NOT to live a smooth life, but to reflect You.*

Sometimes that will cost us. (It cost me over $100!) And sometimes it will be uncomfortable. But if we want others to see God in the mirror of our lives, we need to ask ourselves, "What would Jesus do?"

WHAT A DIFFERENCE!

There's a book by Charles Sheldon called *In His Steps*. Maybe you're familiar with it. If not, I encourage you to read it. It's a classic that's been around for a long time. But the message is as fresh today as when it was written.

The pastor of a small church challenges his congregation to spend an entire year asking themselves, "What would Jesus do?" It changed the history of that church. And more importantly, it *transformed* individuals within the church. It impacted the community. I won't spoil the story—you've got to read it yourself. (A contemporary version, *What Would Jesus Do?* by Garrett Sheldon, also is available.)

Casual Christians will never ask themselves that question. And the world will never see Jesus in the lives of half-way committed disciples. Cheryl possessed the kingdom of God. Susan was saturated with the Lord. Carman is living out his faith. Mature Christians. Deeply committed disciples. People who *glow* with the Lord.

I've often thought back on that hot, hectic day in the Los Angeles airport when my patience was wearing thin. Was God testing me? What if I had simply referred the frantic woman to a flight attendant? Would I have failed the test? Even though it cost me financially, I'm glad I took the time to be "Jesus" to someone around me.

Speaking of passing and failing . . . check out this true story by Bernice Brooks.

THE FINAL I FAILED

Finals week had arrived with all its stress. I had been up late cramming for an exam. Now, as I slumped in my seat, I felt like a spring that had been wound too tight. I had two tests back-to-back, and I was anxious to get through with them. At the same time I expected to be able to maintain my straight-A grade-point average.

As I waited impatiently for the professor to arrive, a stranger walked up to the blackboard and began to write.

"Due to a conflict, your professor is unable to give you your test in this classroom. He is waiting for you in the gymnasium."

Oh, great, I thought. *Now I have to walk clear across campus just to take this stupid exam.*

The entire class was scurrying out the door and rushing to the gym. No one wanted to be late for the final, and we weren't wasting time talking.

The route to the gym took us past the hospital. There was a man stumbling around in front of it. I recognized him as the young blind man whose wife had just given birth to a baby in that hospital. He had been there before, but he must have become confused.

Oh, well, I told myself. *Someone will come along soon and help him. I just don't have time to stop now.*

So I hurried along with the rest of the class on our way to take that final exam.

As we continued down the sidewalk, a woman came rushing out of a nearby bookstore. She had a baby on one arm, a stack of books on the other, and a worried look on her face. The books fell onto the sidewalk, and the baby began to cry as she stooped to pick them up.

She should have left that kid at home, I thought. I dodged her as the class and I rushed along.

Just around the next corner someone had left a dog on a leash tied to a tree. He was a big, friendly mutt, and we had all seen him there before, but today he couldn't quite reach the pan of water left for him. He was straining at his leash and whining.

I thought, *What cruel pet owner would tie up a dog and not leave his water where he could reach it?* But I hurried on.

As we neared the gym, a car passed us and parked close to the door. I recognized the man who got out as one of the maintenance crew. I also noticed he left the lights on. "He's going to have a problem when he tries to start that car to go home tonight," the fellow next to me said.

By that time we were going in the doors of the gym. The maintenance man waved a greeting to us and disappeared down one of the halls. We found seats close to where our teacher waited.

The professor stood with his arms folded, looking at us. We looked back. The silence became uncomfortable. We all knew his tests were also teaching tools, and we wondered what he was up to. He motioned toward the door, and in walked the blind man, the young mother with her baby, a girl holding the big dog on a leash, and the maintenance man.

These people had been planted along the way in an effort to test whether or not the class had grasped the meaning behind the story of the man who fell among thieves. We all failed.[1]

STUFF YOU DON'T HAVE TO PRAY ABOUT

Settled: It's pretty clear that Jesus wants to live through us, isn't it? Do you really need to spend time praying about whether to reach out to those around you. Nah.

Even when there's a price involved—your time, your money, your freedom—the call remains the same: Be Jesus to those around you.

STUFF YOU SHOULD PRAY ABOUT

Again, God isn't pleased with casual Christians. He can't use people as well who are committed 50 percent. Or 68 percent. Or even 92 percent. God needs 100 percent, sold-out, totally committed disciples to impact the world. So pray:

1. That the Holy Spirit will fill your life. When someone is really sold out to Christ, the world can't help but notice. The Holy Spirit is God's personality living in and through you. To be a Spirit-filled Christian means you have completely yielded to Him. Totally surrendered. Made Him Lord of your life. Giving up your way and letting God have His way in you.

Ammunition: Galatians 2:20. What happens when we "die" to ourselves? What kind of difference will others notice in your life when you "die" to your own way?

2. That the Holy Spirit will control your life. When we allow the Holy Spirit to be in the driver's seat, we automatically take the back seat. He moves into the master room, and we take the guest room. This means our desires no longer control us—but the fruit of His Spirit shines through us.

Ammunition: Galatians 5:19–23. Notice the big difference between *our* desires and *His* fruit? Try to memorize all the fruits of the Spirit this week.

3. That the Holy Spirit's power will guide your life. If the Holy Spirit reigns, His power will be evidenced in all you do: your decisions, your conversations, your friendships.

Ammunition: Galatians 5:24–26. How will your life change when the Holy Spirit's power flows through you?

> **Father, I don't want to simply CALL You Lord. I want You to BE Lord. So right now, I give You the reigns to my life. YOU take the driver's seat. I'm just a passenger—YOUR passenger.**
>
> **Jesus, I give You permission to use me like clay in Your hands. Shape me, mold me, remake me in Your image. I'm dying to myself and coming alive to Your will, Your way, Your authority.**
>
> **Now help me to live by Your power . . . and not my own. In Your name I pray, Amen.**

Notes

1. *Permission granted from Judson Press to reprint "The Final I Failed" by Bernice Brooks.*

STUFF TO GROW ON #9

Stuff Jesus Has Been Praying for YOU!

Isn't it exciting to know that the Creator of the universe has been praying for *you*? Would you like to know what He's been saying about you? I've paraphrased the prayer Jesus prayed in John 17. I've used the pronoun *him*, as a generic term. Cross out and put *her* if you want, and please write your own name in the blanks provided.

Here it is:

Father, (insert your name) is my personal glory. I glow when I think of him. That's because I love him as if he were the only one in all the world to love. I believe in his potential. I see *so much* in his life. I'm excited about all You have in store for him.

Keep him close to You, Father. Help _____ realize that You and I dream B-I-G dreams for him. I ask You to take extra good care of him. Those days when he feels like the whole world is against him, and no one understands, let him sit in Your lap—just like a child.

Wrap Your strong arms of love around him and wipe his tears away.

Sometimes, Father, he doesn't show his tears. Sometimes he does all his crying on the inside. Help him feel comfortable enough around You to ACT on what he's FEELING.

He's so hard on himself . . . times when he's his own worst enemy—beating himself up over not meeting someone's expectation. Teach him that YOUR expectations are what's *really* important in life.

He's so much fun, Lord. I love laughing with _____. Sometimes we just talk about *daily* stuff—like who's spreading rumors about him, his latest grade in math class, trying to get so-and-so to notice him. And You know what? I love it! I'm glad he knows there's absolutely NOTHING too big or too small to pray about. I'm thrilled he knows that We care about *everything!*

I'm concerned about unity, Father. I want _____ to live in harmony and peace with those around him. Help him to get over this feeling of having to be right all the time. Help Me teach him humility and genuine concern for others. I crave unity between My children . . . I want them to have the same kind of oneness that You and I have.

Keep him safe. Protect him. We'll walk by his side together, Father. We'll take each step he takes, and We'll feel everything he feels. The good AND the bad. The laughter, the pain, the aloneness, the confusion, the joy. I want to experience all that *with* him.

I've told him a lot—even wrote it all down for him . . . a personal collection of letters. I hope he listens. I'm going to keep talking to him—leading him and guiding him—through the Spirit that I'll pour inside of him, and through My letters. I'm concerned that he hear and understand My voice. If he'll just read My letters, everything will make sense. Help him do that, Father. And assist him in being consistent in getting to know Us.

The world hates _____. They hate him because he doesn't really fit in. And I'm glad he's not fitting in, because he's really no more a part of this world than I am. But he has a hard time understanding that. Sometimes he wants to fit in—forgetting that his real home is with Us . . . and that it's far beyond his wildest imagination. I wish We could give him a little taste of heaven, Father. But, I know.

That's where faith comes in. Help Me to increase his faith. I want nothing more than for him to become all We dream for him to be.

I'll be joining You soon. And together, We'll work on getting his house ready. In My place, though, I'll leave My very own personality—My Spirit—full of everything I am, for his fulfillment and spiritual success.

I love _____ so much, I'm giving My very *life* for his growth in holiness and truth and understanding. My life for _____. It's worth it, Father. We have a genuine treasure when We have _____.